EXECUTIVE CHEF

Executive Chef

PRINCESS CRUISES CUISINE

The Best Recipes from Princess Cruises' Award-Winning Chefs' Collection

Dorison House Publishers

Boston

ISBN: 916752-66-6

Library of Congress Number: 9C 080035

Published by Dorison House Publishers, Inc.
31 St. James Avenue
Boston, MA 02116

Manufactured in the United States of America

CONTENTS

Stuffed Pears with Walnuts and Gorgonzola Cheese, recipe on page 14.

INTRODUCTION

We at Princess Cruises® are especially proud of our award-winning cuisine. Our chefs prepare their dishes in the belief that cruise passengers should return home having experienced the ultimate in dining pleasure.

We received so many requests from our passengers for the chefs' recipes, that this cookbook has been prepared especially for you. The chefs' choice recipes have been adapted for home cooks so that you can recapture the pleasure of Princess cuisine in your own home, sharing it with your friends and family.

Buon appetito! And we look forward to seeing you again on another Princess cruise.

Pietro Corsi
Princess Cruises
Hotel Services

Princess Cruises' Crown Princess.^{SM}

Opposite page: Supplì al Telefono, recipe on page 7.

APPETIZERS

6

Supplì al Telefono
Parmigiano Delights
Canapé au Fromage
Jalapeño Cheese Dip
Chicken Liver Pâté
Yellow and Red Peperoni Antipasto
Eggplant Marinated Sorrentina
Eggplant Caponata
Lobster Cocktail
Lobster Thermidor
Oysters Rockefeller
Stuffed Pears with Walnuts and Gorgonzola Cheese
Guacamole

Canapé au Fromage, recipe on page 8.

Supplì al Telefono

(RICE CROQUETTES)

This Roman favorite gets its name "croquettes on the telephone" because the melted cheese draws out into long "wires" as it is forked from the plate.

INGREDIENTS:

1 small onion, chopped
3 tablespoons butter
1 cup uncooked rice
4 ounces dry white wine
1½ cups chicken broth
Pinch each of marjoram, thyme, saffron
¼ cup Parmesan cheese, grated
Salt and pepper to taste
2 eggs, lightly beaten
4 ounces mozzarella cheese, cut in small cubes
1 cup plain bread crumbs
1 cup vegetable oil

PREPARATION:

In a saucepan at medium heat, sauté the onion in butter until it is transparent. Add the rice and stir for 1 minute. Add wine and cook until it has evaporated. Add chicken broth and herbs.

Simmer for 20 minutes, stirring occasionally until the rice is done and the liquid has evaporated. Add Parmesan cheese, salt, pepper and the eggs. Stir well to blend; allow to cool.

Scoop up about a tablespoon of risotto and place it in your hand. Place a cube of cheese in the middle of it, then top it with another tablespoonful of risotto. Press to shape a ball. (The balls may be fried at once, but they are easier to handle if they are refrigerated for 30 minutes.)

Heat the oil in a deep skillet to 375 degrees. Dip each ball in bread crumbs and fry them 8 at a time for 4 or 5 minutes, turning them occasionally, until they are golden brown and the cheese has melted. Transfer to paper towels to drain. Then arrange them in a baking dish. They may be kept warm in the oven, for not more than 10 minutes, until you are ready to serve.

Serve plain or with Fresh Tomato Sauce (see page 77).

4 Servings. Makes 16 pieces.

Parmigiano Delights

INGREDIENTS:

1 cup Parmesan cheese, grated
1 cup mayonnaise
2 tablespoons Worcestershire sauce
1 onion, minced
3 ounces dry sherry

PREPARATION:

Blend all ingredients; stir until well mixed. Spread on small slices of cocktail rye bread or crackers; sprinkle with additional Parmesan cheese. Broil until bubbly and lightly browned.

Serve hot.

Makes 2½ cups of cheese spread.

8

CANAPÉ AU FROMAGE

(CHEESE BALLS)

Tasty morsels to be served with crackers.

INGREDIENTS:

½ cup cottage cheese
1 (8-ounce package) cream cheese, softened
2 tablespoons chopped parsley
1 tablespoon sherry
1 tablespoon Dijon mustard
½ teaspoon salt
Dash of Tabasco sauce
1¼ cups walnuts, chopped

PREPARATION:

Mix together cottage cheese and cream cheese, add parsley, sherry, mustard and condiments. Chill for 1 hour.

Shape the mixture into 1-inch balls. Roll the balls in chopped nuts until they are completely covered.

Place them in the refrigerator to chill.

Makes 30.

JALAPEÑO CHEESE DIP

This is perfect cocktail fare to have on hand for unexpected guests.

INGREDIENTS:

1 jalapeño pepper
1 tablespoon medium hot green chili peppers
1 scallion
½ pound cream cheese, cut into ½-inch pieces
6 ounces sharp Cheddar cheese, cut into ½-inch pieces
Dash of Tabasco sauce
Dash of Worcestershire sauce
Salt and cayenne pepper to taste
4 tablespoons cold milk

PREPARATION:

In the container of a blender or food processor, mince jalapeño pepper, green chili peppers and scallion. Add the rest of the ingredients and purée until smooth and soft.

Refrigerate for at least 1 hour before serving.

Makes 2 cups.

CHICKEN LIVER PÂTÉ

A savory appetizer. Smooth as silk to contrast with the crispness of the toast or crackers.

INGREDIENTS:

¼ cup butter
2 small onions, chopped
2 cloves garlic, minced
8 ounces chicken livers, rinsed and drained
Salt and pepper to taste
1 ounce dry sherry
1 ounce brandy
½ teaspoon Worcestershire sauce
2 hard-cooked eggs, chopped

PREPARATION:

In a large, heavy skillet, melt 2 tablespoons of the butter; add onion and garlic. Sauté until golden. Add the chicken livers and sauté, stirring often until they are just slightly pink, for about 2 minutes. Add salt, pepper, sherry and brandy, and stir and cook for another 2 minutes.

Ladle the chicken liver mixture into the container of a food processor or blender. Purée, a few seconds, until it is smooth.

Transfer the pâté to a mixing bowl. Melt and stir in the remaining butter, Worcestershire sauce and chopped eggs. Turn into a serving dish, cover and chill several hours before serving. The pâté may be spread on melba toast as canapés, or mounded on a serving platter, sprinkled with chopped egg and surrounded with radish roses, crackers and toast.

VARIATION:

Omit the chopped hard-cooked eggs. Cook the liver as per above preparation. Transfer the cooked liver mixture to a food processor.

Using the same skillet, melt the remaining butter. Sauté 2 cups sliced fresh mushrooms until soft. Add mushrooms and 3 ounces of softened cream cheese to the liver mixture. Process until smooth. Stir in Worcestershire sauce. Mix well.

Makes 2 cups.

9

10

YELLOW AND RED PEPERONI ANTIPASTO

"Antipasto" is the Italian word for "before the meal." What goes into it may depend on the imagination of the cook. Here is our Princess Cruises Chefs' suggestion.

INGREDIENTS:

3 large red bell peppers
3 large yellow bell peppers
8 anchovy fillets in oil
1 teaspoon capers, washed and drained
3 tablespoons olive oil
2 tablespoons white vinegar
4 cloves garlic, finely sliced
2 tablespoons chopped parsley
Salt and pepper
Pinch each of thyme and marjoram
12 Kalamata (Greek) black olives
2 hard-cooked eggs, cut into wedges

PREPARATION:

To roast the peppers:

Preheat the oven to 400 degrees. Bake the peppers for 35 minutes, turning them twice. Allow them to cool, remove the skin and seeds and cut them in strips.

On each serving plate, place some peppers of each color in the center. Top with anchovy fillets and capers. Mix oil and vinegar with garlic, parsley and seasoning. Pour the dressing over the top.

Garnish with egg wedges and black olives.

4 Servings.

Yellow and Red Peperoni Antipasto.

EGGPLANT MARINATED SORRENTINA

11

This Sicilian eggplant mixture may be served as part of the Antipasto Platter or on its own. Covered with oil and refrigerated, it can be kept for two weeks.

INGREDIENTS:

1 large and firm eggplant
½ cup water
3 tablespoons fresh Italian parsley, chopped
4 cloves garlic, minced
¼ teaspoon oregano
¼ teaspoon marjoram
Salt and freshly ground pepper to taste
6 tablespoons olive oil
3 tablespoons wine vinegar

PREPARATION:

Preheat the oven to 400 degrees. In a 9-inch baking pan, bake the whole eggplant with the skin intact, adding ½ cup water to the pan. Cook for 15 minutes and turn it over. Return the eggplant to the oven for another 15 minutes or until it is soft and the skin is almost dry and separated from the pulp.

Remove the pan from the oven. Cut the eggplant in half and stand it on end to drain the remaining liquid; let it cool.

Peel, seed, and cut the eggplant into ¼-inch strips. Place a layer of the strips in a soup plate or bowl and sprinkle it with mixture of parsley, garlic clove, oregano, marjoram, salt and pepper. Repeat the layering. Finally, pour oil and vinegar over the top. Set it aside for a few hours; serve it at room temperature with pita bread.

4 Servings (1¾ cups).

12

EGGPLANT CAPONATA

This zesty Sicilian dish is usually served cold as an appetizer, but it may be served as a complement to broiled swordfish steak.

INGREDIENTS:

½ cup olive oil
2 medium-sized eggplants, peeled and cut into ¾-inch cubes
1 small onion, chopped
1 rib celery, chopped
2 small tomatoes, chopped
1 tablespoon granulated sugar
3 tablespoons vinegar
½ teaspoon salt
¼ teaspoon ground black pepper
1 teaspoon capers, washed and drained
3 tablespoons sultana raisins
2 tablespoons pine nuts

PREPARATION:

In a 12-inch skillet, warm the oil and sauté the eggplant until it is crispy and brown.

Remove 2 tablespoons of the oil to another skillet and cook the onion and celery until they are transparent. Add tomatoes and stir; cook for 2 minutes. Add the sugar, vinegar, salt and pepper; bring to a boil for 1 minute. Finally, stir in the eggplant.

Mound the mixture on a serving plate, and garnish with the mixture of capers, raisins and pine nuts.

6 Servings.

LOBSTER COCKTAIL

Lobster, shrimp or crabmeat can be used in this spicy dish.

INGREDIENTS:

3 tablespoons mayonnaise
2 tablespoons chili sauce
1 teaspoon Worcestershire sauce
1 tablespoon chopped chives
1 tablespoon chopped parsley
2 small tomatoes, peeled, seeded and finely chopped
1 cup cooked lobster meat, cut in small pieces
3 tablespoons diced celery
3 tablespoons chopped lettuce hearts
Salad greens
1 lemon

PREPARATION:

In a bowl, combine mayonnaise, chili sauce, Worcestershire sauce, chives, parsley and tomatoes; mix well. Add the lobster meat, celery and chopped lettuce hearts.

Serve the salad on a bed of greens. Garnish with a lemon wedge.

4 Servings.

LOBSTER THERMIDOR

This can be served either as a first course or luncheon dish.

INGREDIENTS:

**5 tablespoons butter
½ cup chopped mushrooms
1 tablespoon Worcestershire sauce
1 tablespoon freshly chopped parsley
2 teaspoons chopped pimiento
3 pounds cooked fresh lobster meat
⅓ cup bread crumbs
3 ounces dry sherry
1 ounce brandy
1 cup heavy cream
3 egg yolks
4 tablespoons grated Swiss cheese
2 teaspoons paprika**

PREPARATION:

Preheat the oven to 400 degrees.

In a medium-sized saucepan, heat 3 tablespoons of the butter, add mushrooms and cook for 5 minutes. Add Worcestershire sauce, parsley, pimiento, lobster meat, bread crumbs, sherry, brandy, cream and egg yolks. Mix well.

Fill individual casseroles or sea shells with the mixture. Sprinkle with cheese, dot with the remaining butter, and sprinkle with paprika. Bake for 15 minutes. Serve immediately.

4 Servings.

OYSTERS ROCKEFELLER

Oysters set the tone for an elegant dinner.

INGREDIENTS:

**2 tablespoons minced onion
3 tablespoons minced celery
4 tablespoons butter
4 tablespoons minced spinach
2 tablespoons minced parsley
4 tablespoons bread crumbs
¼ teaspoon Tabasco sauce
Pinch of salt
12 oysters in half shell, freshly opened and
    drained**

PREPARATION:

Preheat the oven to 350 degrees.

In a large skillet, sauté onion and celery in butter until the onion is transparent. Add spinach, parsley, bread crumbs, Tabasco sauce and salt, if desired.

Top each oyster with the mixture. You should have 1 teaspoon for each small oyster half, or 2 teaspoons each for large oyster halves. Arrange the filled oysters in a baking pan lined with rock salt or table salt and bake for 10 minutes.

4 Servings.

14

STUFFED PEARS WITH WALNUTS AND GORGONZOLA CHEESE

Fresh pears go well with the tangy cheese as a first course. (See photograph on page 3.)

INGREDIENTS:

2 ripe, but firm, Bartlett pears
6 ounces pungent Gorgonzola cheese, softened
2 tablespoons cream cheese
4 tablespoons chopped walnuts
1 ounce dry sherry
2 cups shredded lettuce

PREPARATION:

Wash the pears, but do not peel them. Slice them lengthwise in half and remove the cores with an apple corer, leaving the stems on.

Combine the Gorgonzola and cream cheese. Stir in half the walnuts and all of the sherry. Use this mixture to fill the pears.

Arrange shredded lettuce as nests on chilled serving plates. Place a stuffed pear half in each nest. Garnish with the remainder of the chopped nuts.

CHEF'S TIP:

For color appeal, you may garnish each serving with assorted berries in season or red grapes.

4 Servings.

GUACAMOLE

The chili peppers give this popular avocado dip a little added zip.

INGREDIENTS:

2 medium-sized ripe avocados, peeled and cut up
1 medium-sized onion, finely chopped
2 green chili peppers, ribs and seeds removed, finely chopped
2 tablespoons lemon juice
½ teaspoon salt
½ teaspoon ground pepper
1 medium-sized ripe tomato, finely chopped

PREPARATION:

In a medium-sized bowl, whisk avocados, onion, chili peppers, lemon juice, salt and pepper until creamy. Stir in tomato. Refrigerate for at least 1 hour before serving with a bowl of corn chips.

CHEF'S TIP:

To keep, refrigerate the dip, tightly covered with plastic wrap. Be sure it is touching the guacamole to prevent the air from turning it dark. (Some "weeping" may occur when held for 24 hours. Drain off the liquid and discard it.)

Makes 2¾ cups.

Opposite page: Avgolemono Soup, recipe on page 17.

Soups

16

Sopa de Frijol Negro (Black Bean Soup), recipe on opposite page.

Avgolemono Soup

This is a traditional Greek soup with a delicate lemon flavor and a sunny appearance. It is surprisingly simple to make, considering how delicious it is.

INGREDIENTS:

4 tablespoons uncooked rice
5 cups chicken or lamb broth
4 eggs
Juice of 2 lemons
Salt to taste

PREPARATION:

In a large saucepan, cook rice in broth for 25 minutes.

In a separate bowl, combine eggs and lemon juice; beat for 2 minutes.

Remove the broth from heat; whisk in the egg mixture. Divide the soup among 4 bowls and serve immediately.

The soup should be creamy but not too thick.

4 Servings.

Sopa de Frijol Negro

(BLACK BEAN SOUP)

A great soup. It freezes well and it is worthwhile to make in large quantities.

INGREDIENTS:

6 cups water
4 ounces dried black beans
½ pound ham shank or smoked pork hocks
1 clove garlic, finely chopped
1 bay leaf
¼ teaspoon crushed dried chili pepper
1 medium-sized carrot, sliced
1 medium-sized celery rib, chopped
1 medium-sized onion, chopped
2 tablespoons white vinegar
2 hard-cooked eggs, finely chopped

PREPARATION:

In a large pot, heat water, beans and pork to boiling. Then reduce the heat, cover and simmer for about 2 hours or until the beans are tender. Stir in garlic, bay leaf, chili pepper, carrot, celery and onion. Cover and simmer for another hour.

Remove pork to cool, and dice for garnish. Discard the bay leaf. Ladle the soup into a blender container, add the white vinegar and blend until it is smooth.

Reheat before serving the soup, garnished with diced pork and finely chopped hard-cooked eggs.

4 Servings.

PETITE MARMITE

This soup was invented more than 80 years ago in France and has become popular in both Europe and America.

INGREDIENTS:

½ **pound lean beef, cut in chunks**
½ **boneless chicken, cut up**
2 quarts beef stock
1 leek, sliced, white part only
1 small onion, sliced
¼ **small white cabbage, sliced**
1 carrot, cubed
1 small turnip, cubed
½ **celery root, sliced**
Salt and freshly ground pepper

PREPARATION:

In a heavy, covered pot, simmer the beef and chicken in the beef stock until tender, then remove the meat and let it cool. Bring the liquid to a slow boil. Add all the vegetables to the pot and simmer for 10 minutes.

Cut the chicken and beef into small cubes and return them to the pot. Cook for 15 more minutes; add salt and pepper if needed.

Serve with thin slices of toast.

4 Servings.

MULLIGATAWNY SOUP

From India, we have this wonderfully flavored soup. "Mulligatawny" comes from the Tamil word milakutanni, *meaning pepper water.*

INGREDIENTS:

1 small onion, chopped
1 medium-sized carrot, chopped
1 turnip, peeled and chopped
1 apple, peeled and chopped
3 tablespoons butter or margarine
2 tablespoons all-purpose flour
1 tablespoon curry powder
3 cups chicken stock or broth
½ **pound chicken breast, cut in small cubes**
Bouquet garni (bay leaf, parsley, thyme)
1 tablespoon lemon juice
½ **cup heavy cream**
Salt and pepper
4 tablespoons steamed fluffy rice (pre-cooked)

PREPARATION:

In a 2-quart pot, sauté onion, carrot, turnip and apple in butter or margarine until limp and slightly colored. Stir in flour and curry powder; then add chicken stock. Finally, add the cubed chicken, and the bouquet garni. Simmer, covered, for 1½ hours.

Strain the soup; add lemon juice and cream. Serve hot or chilled, garnished with fluffy rice.

4 Servings.

New England Clam Chowder

The clams in the recipe may be called "steamers" or "long necks."

INGREDIENTS:

2 dozen medium-sized hard-shelled clams
3 cups cold water
2 ounces salt pork, diced
1 small onion, chopped
Salt and freshly ground black pepper to taste
2 medium-sized potatoes, diced
1 cup milk
½ cup light cream

PREPARATION:

Wash the clams thoroughly. Place them in a deep saucepan with the cold water; bring to a boil and simmer gently for 10 minutes, or until the shells open. The water should almost cover the clams.

Strain the broth through cheesecloth and reserve. Remove the shells and chop the clam meat.

Fry the salt pork in the deep saucepan. Add the onion and cook slowly until it begins to turn golden brown. Add the clams and the reserved broth. Skim, if necessary.

Add the potatoes and season with salt and pepper. Cook until the potatoes are tender.

Remove the mixture from the heat, slowly add the milk and cream, which have been heated. Serve immediately in large warmed soup bowls. Serve with crackers, if desired.

4 Servings.

Corn Chowder

This is an easy, excellent recipe for an American favorite.

INGREDIENTS:

2 tablespoons salt pork, diced
1 tablespoon onion, finely chopped
1½ cups water
1 bay leaf, sprigs of sage and parsley
2 medium-sized potatoes, peeled and diced
2 cups milk
1 cup corn kernels
2 egg yolks, beaten
1 tablespoon melted butter
1 teaspoon paprika

PREPARATION:

In a saucepan, brown the salt pork and onion. Add the water, bay leaf, sage, parsley and potatoes and bring to a boil. Cover and cook until potatoes are tender.

Stir in the milk and corn and cook for 5 minutes. In the meantime, beat the egg yolks with a wire whisk and combine them with the melted butter. Slowly stir a small amount of the chowder mixture into the egg mixture, stirring until blended. Pour the egg mixture slowly into the chowder, stirring constantly.

To serve, ladle hot chowder into soup bowls and sprinkle with paprika.

4 Servings.

20

MINESTRONE GENOVESE

Genovese prefer this soup thick.

INGREDIENTS:

½ pound fresh spinach washed, drained and
   chopped
1 cup pinto beans, fresh or canned
¼ cup cauliflower flowerets
½ cup fresh peas
4 squash flowers
1 rib celery, chopped
1 small onion, chopped
1 russet potato, diced
1 small zucchini
¼ cup fresh string beans, cut into ½-inch
   pieces
2 quarts water
5 ounces linguine, crushed
Salt to taste
½ cup Pesto Sauce
2 tablespoons olive oil

PREPARATION:

In a deep pot, combine all ingredients
except the linguine, salt, olive oil, and Pesto
Sauce.

Bring the soup to a boil. Reduce the
heat and simmer until the vegetables are tender.
Add more water, if the soup is too thick. Add
pasta and cook for 15 minutes. Season to taste.

Add the Pesto Sauce and olive oil just 5
minutes before serving. Serve with crusty bread
and butter.

4 Servings.

PESTO SAUCE:

(BASIL SAUCE)

INGREDIENTS:

1 cup fresh basil leaves, washed and drained
   only
6 tablespoons freshly grated Parmesan cheese
4 tablespoons olive oil
3 tablespoons pine nuts (pignola nuts)
5 cloves garlic
2 tablespoons dairy sour cream

PREPARATION:

In a blender or food processor, blend all
ingredients together for 3 or more minutes to
obtain a thick green sauce (enough for 4 servings
of pasta or gnocchis).

Makes 1 cup.

POTAGE ST. GERMAINE

(SPLIT PEA SOUP)

*Add a cup of fresh cooked and puréed green peas
after the soup has been strained.*

INGREDIENTS:

½ pound dried split green peas
2 quarts cold water
4 tablespoons diced salt pork
1 chopped leek
1 stalk celery, chopped
1 small onion, chopped
1 bay leaf
1 pig's knuckle
Salt to taste
1 smoked Dutch ring sausage, sliced
2 tablespoons chopped parsley

PREPARATION:

Rinse the peas under cold water and pick them over to remove all foreign particles. Place the peas in a kettle, add the water, cover and let stand overnight.

In a skillet, cook the salt pork for 5 minutes. Add the vegetables and cook for 10 minutes, until tender but not browned.

Add the salt pork mixture, bay leaf, pig's knuckle and salt to the peas. Cover and bring slowly to a boil. Reduce the heat, skim foam from the top and simmer for 2 hours, or until the meat on the pig's knuckle separates from the bone.

Remove the pig's knuckle, shred the meat and reserve. Discard the bone and the bay leaf.

Strain the soup and press the vegetables through a sieve. Return the meat and sieved vegetables to the soup kettle and adjust the seasonings. Add the sliced sausages and simmer for 5 minutes longer.

Serve the soup piping hot and garnish each portion with chopped parsley.

4 Servings.

CREAM OF CAULIFLOWER SOUP

A satisfyingly flavorful soup.

INGREDIENTS:

**4 tablespoons butter
1 leek, white part only, finely chopped
1 medium-sized carrot, finely chopped
1 pound cauliflower, flowerets only
½ teaspoon dried thyme
½ cup dry white wine
3 cups chicken stock
½ cup light cream, at room temperature
Salt and freshly ground black pepper
2 tablespoons anise flavored liqueur, such as Anisette or Sambuca**

PREPARATION:

Melt the butter in a heavy saucepan. Add the leek, carrot and cauliflower and sauté until the vegetables are tender.

Add the thyme, wine and chicken stock and bring to a boil. Lower the heat and simmer, covered, for 40 minutes.

Remove the soup from the heat and purée it in a blender or food processor. Pour the purée into the top of a double boiler. Pour a ladleful of the hot soup into the cream, and then pour the mixture back into the soup. Add salt and pepper to taste. Stir in the liqueur. Serve hot or chilled with crisp bread sticks.

4 Servings.

22

CRÈME VICHYSSOISE

(CREAM OF POTATO SOUP)

Simply by transforming potato soup to vichyssoise, *it becomes an epicure's delight.*

INGREDIENTS:

2 leeks, chopped, white part only
1 medium onion, chopped
4 tablespoons butter
3 medium-sized potatoes, peeled and thinly
    sliced
2 cups chicken broth
½ cup watercress, leaves only
2 cups milk
1 cup heavy cream
Salt, if needed

PREPARATION:

In a deep kettle, lightly brown the leek and onion in butter. Add potatoes, broth and watercress and simmer for 40 minutes. Drain, reserving liquid.

In the container of a blender or food processor, purée the cooked vegetables until they are smooth. Return the purée to the kettle, add the reserved liquid, milk and cream. Taste for salt. Stir, cover and refrigerate.

Serve hot or cold with a garnish of freshly chopped chives.

4 Servings.

COLD SHRIMP AND TOMATO BISQUE

In the vocabulary of soups, a cream soup in which the main ingredient is shellfish may be called a bisque. Whatever you call it, this is the best.

INGREDIENTS:

3 tablespoons butter
4 tablespoons all-purpose flour
4 cups fish stock (see page 49)
1 pound shrimp, shelled and deveined
1 tablespoon tomato paste
1 tablespoon curry powder
½ cup light cream
Pimiento strips, tomato slices and halved
    shrimp, for garnish

PREPARATION:

In a large saucepan, melt the butter, stir in flour and gradually add the fish stock. Bring the stock to a boil, reduce heat and simmer for 15 minutes, stirring constantly.

Cook the shrimp in boiling salted water for 5 minutes. Save 4 whole shrimp for garnish. Drain the rest of the shrimp and purée them in a blender or food processor, using about ¾ cup of the stock to moisten them. Add tomato paste to the shrimp purée and combine it with the remaining fish stock, blending well. Stir in curry powder and light cream.

Cool the soup and chill it.

Garnish each serving with thin pimiento strips, tomato slices and halved cooked shrimp.

4 Servings.

Cold Shrimp and Tomato Bisque, recipe on opposite page.

24 POTAGE CRÈME D'ASPERGES

(CHILLED CREAM OF ASPARAGUS SOUP)

Float some cooked asparagus tips on top of the soup. It helps to identify the type of vegetable used and gives it some texture.

INGREDIENTS:

4 tablespoons butter
1 small onion, chopped
2 ribs celery, chopped
1 pound fresh tender asparagus spears, cut into 1-inch pieces
3 cups milk
1 cup half-and-half
Salt, pepper and nutmeg
Lemon peel, grated

PREPARATION:

In a saucepan, melt butter and sauté the onion and celery until light brown. Add asparagus and milk and simmer until the asparagus is tender.

In a blender, food mill or processor, purée the soup until it is smooth. Refrigerate for at least 2 hours, then add the half-and-half just before serving. Taste for seasoning, and add salt, pepper and nutmeg as needed. Garnish with grated lemon peel.

4 Servings.

Tortue Jellied Consommé, recipe on opposite page.

TORTUE JELLIED CONSOMMÉ

A French West Indies icy soup for a chic dinner party. For best results, this should be prepared the day before serving.

INGREDIENTS:

4 ounces white fish, chopped
1 small ripe tomato, halved
Bouquet garni (celery, thyme, bay leaf)
½ cup dry white wine
3½ cups water
1 teaspoon vinegar
Salt to taste
1 package clear gelatin
4 tablespoons dairy sour cream
1 ounce Beluga caviar
6 sprigs fresh dill

PREPARATION:

In a medium-sized saucepan, combine fish, tomato, herbs, wine, 3¼ cups of water, vinegar and salt. Cover, bring it to a boil, reduce the heat and simmer slowly for 30 minutes. Periodically, skim off the scum as it rises to the surface. Continue to simmer for another 30 minutes, skimming as often as necessary.

Soften the gelatin in ¼ cup of cold water and stir into the hot stock.

Line a metal strainer with a napkin that has been rinsed in cold water. Strain the consommé through that into a container and then ladle it into individual soup cups. Refrigerate the cups until the consommé is firm.

To serve, top each cup with a tablespoon of sour cream, a dab of caviar and a sprig of fresh dill.

4 Servings.

26

CHILLED GAZPACHO SOUP

This tangy Spanish soup should be prepared six to eight hours before serving to be sure it's ice cold.

INGREDIENTS:

1 pound plum tomatoes (about 6), peeled and seeded
1 small red onion, peeled and quartered
1 green bell pepper, cored and halved
1 medium-sized cucumber, peeled and seeded
1 jalapeño chili pepper, seeded
2 or 3 garlic cloves, peeled
Dash of salt
1 tablespoon red wine vinegar
3 tablespoons olive oil
½ cup cold water
1 cup tomato juice
1 teaspoon lemon juice
Dairy sour cream for garnish

PREPARATION:

In the bowl of a food processor, finely chop each of the first 6 ingredients separately. Transfer to a large jar. Add the remaining ingredients, except the sour cream, to the jar; then, stir to blend and refrigerate.

Serve in chilled bowls with a dollop of sour cream or, for added crunch, pass freshly chopped tomato, red onion, green and red pepper, cucumber and small croutons.

4 Servings.

CHILLED COCONUT YOGURT CREAM SOUP

The yogurt base is very good for quick, refreshing cold soups.

INGREDIENTS:

2 cups plain yogurt
1 cup coconut milk
1 tablespoon honey
1 tablespoon brandy
Orange juice
Toasted coconut flakes and sprigs of mint leaves for garnish

PREPARATION:

In a food processor or blender, combine the yogurt, coconut milk, honey and brandy. Adjust the taste and consistency of the soup by adding orange juice.

Chill thoroughly for at least 1 hour before serving.

Serve garnished with toasted coconut flakes and sprigs of fresh mint leaves.

4 Servings.

Opposite page: Risotto alla Milanese, recipe on page 30.

PASTA AND RICE

28

Cannelloni Gastronomique
Risotto alla Milanese
Linguine Amatriciana
Linguine Pescatóre
Seafood with Spaghetti, Captain Morgan
Vermicelli with Shrimp in Curried Yogurt
Fettucine Monte Carlo
Gnocchi alla Romana
Potato Gnocchi
Spaghetti Aglio e Olio
Spaghetti Scarpara
Party Gourmet Spaghetti
Fusilli or Pasta Primavera
Penne Provençale Salad
Penne alla Carbonara
Baked Macaroni with Ricotta
Tagliatelle with Walnut Sauce

Cannelloni Gastronomique, recipe on opposite page.

CANNELLONI GASTRONOMIQUE

These are crêpes with minced chicken filling. They are not difficult to prepare and are very tasty.

BATTER:

INGREDIENTS:

1½ cups milk
6 eggs
½ teaspoon salt
Dash of nutmeg
1 cup all-purpose flour
2 ounces bacon fat

PREPARATION:

Stir together milk, eggs, salt and nutmeg. Add the flour in small amounts and blend with a wire whisk. Set aside for an hour.

To make the crêpes, heat bacon fat in a 6-inch skillet until it is very hot. Pour about 2 tablespoons of the batter into the pan; rotate the pan so the batter covers the bottom. Pour any excess back into the mixing bowl. Cook about 1 minute. Then lift the edge of the crêpe and turn it over. Cook second side until brown — about 15 seconds. Slide the crêpe onto a plate. (The crêpe should be paper-thin; if it is not, add up to ¼ cup of additional milk to the batter.) Repeat this procedure with remaining batter and set aside.

CHICKEN FILLING:

INGREDIENTS:

¼ cup butter
1 leek, chopped, white part only
1 pound skinned and boned chicken meat, chopped
6 tablespoons dry white wine
1 cup spinach, chopped
4 ounces prosciutto ham, chopped
1 tablespoon dry Porcini mushrooms, soaked and chopped
¼ cup Parmesan cheese
2 large eggs, beaten
Salt and pepper to taste
Dash marjoram and nutmeg
½ cup light cream

PREPARATION:

Preheat the oven to 400 degrees.

In a large skillet, heat the butter and sauté the leek for 5 minutes. Add the chicken and cook for 10 minutes. Stir in wine, spinach, prosciutto and mushrooms. Simmer over medium heat for 15 more minutes.

Remove from heat. Add 4 tablespoons of the cheese, eggs and seasoning. Spoon about ¼ cup of filling onto the center of each cannelloni and roll them up carefully. Place them in a buttered baking dish. Cover with cream, dust with the remaining cheese and bake for 15 minutes.

4 Servings.

30

RISOTTO ALLA MILANESE

This rice dish may be served as an entrée as is, or you can add shrimp, a few slices of Porcini mushrooms, asparagus, or a simple tomato or meat sauce. The saffron is what makes this risotto "Milanese."

INGREDIENTS:

½ cup butter
¼ cup chopped onion
1 cup imported Italian rice (Arborio)
3 cups chicken stock
2 tablespoons beef bone marrow (optional)
Pinch of nutmeg
1 cup dry white wine
½ teaspoon saffron, crushed
½ cup grated Parmesan cheese
Salt to taste

PREPARATION:

In a large skillet, melt 4 tablespoons of the butter and sauté the onion until brown. Add rice and stir for a few seconds. Add the chicken stock; reduce the heat and slowly cook the rice for 15 minutes (do not stir).

Add the bone marrow, nutmeg, wine and saffron. Cook for 7 to 10 more minutes, remove from heat; add the remaining butter and cheese and salt, if needed. Stir well and serve.

4 Servings.

LINGUINE AMATRICIANA

The Sabine town of Amatrice has given its name to this spaghetti sauce, a specialty of the Italian table that's easy to prepare and very tasty.

INGREDIENTS:

2 tablespoons olive oil
1 tablespoon unsalted butter
2 cloves garlic, crushed
1 medium-sized onion, finely chopped
6 leaves fresh basil
3 ounces slab bacon, finely sliced
1 pound fresh ripe plum tomatoes, peeled,
    seeded and chopped
Salt and freshly ground pepper
12 ounces linguine
4 tablespoons freshly grated Romano or
    pecorino cheese

PREPARATION:

Heat oil and butter in a heavy medium-sized saucepan over medium heat. When foam subsides, add garlic and sauté, shaking pan frequently, until garlic is golden brown. Remove and discard garlic. Add onion, basil and bacon to the oil. Sauté for a few minutes stirring occasionally, until onion begins to turn golden. Add tomatoes and bring the mixture to a boil. Reduce the heat to low and allow the sauce to simmer for about 15 minutes, until it thickens. Season to taste with salt and pepper.

Cook pasta in a large saucepan of lightly salted boiling water over high heat until just "*al dente*," about 7 to 10 minutes. Drain thoroughly and transfer to a warmed serving bowl.

Pour the sauce over the pasta. Toss it at the table. Sprinkle with cheese.

4 Servings.

LINGUINE PESCATÓRE

(PASTA WITH SEAFOOD, TOMATOES AND HERBS)

Spaghetti should be tender, but still firm to the bite — in Italian, al dente*. If it is overcooked, it is soft. Serve it steaming hot, as soon as it is cooked.*

INGREDIENTS:

¼ **cup olive oil**
3 garlic cloves, finely chopped
1 onion, finely chopped
3 cups imported plum tomatoes, peeled,
    seeded and chopped
½ **cup fish stock (see page 49)**
2 tablespoons dry white wine
1 tablespoon chopped fresh basil leaves
¼ **teaspoon hot red pepper flakes**
½ **pound scallops**
8 mussels, scrubbed and debearded*
8 shrimps, peeled and deveined
4 littleneck clams, washed
8 tablespoons finely chopped fresh parsley
    leaves
12 ounces spaghetti or linguine

PREPARATION:

Heat the oil in a large saucepan. Add the garlic and onions and sauté until the onion is translucent.

Add the tomatoes, stock, wine, basil and hot pepper flakes to the pan. Simmer for 20 minutes.

Transfer 1 cup of this sauce to another saucepan and poach the scallops in it for about 5 minutes. Do not overcook the fish.

At the same time, add the remaining seafood and 2 tablespoons of the parsley to the sauce. Cover and cook for 10 minutes, or until all the seafood is cooked. Leave the clams and mussels in their shells.

While the seafood is cooking, cook the linguine in boiling salted water until it is *al dente*. Drain the linguine and transfer it to a warm serving bowl.

Place the scallops in the center of the pasta and surround it with the other seafood. Pour the sauce over the top and sprinkle with the remaining parsley.

4 Servings.

———————

* **Note:** *For the technique of cleaning mussels, see the Chef's Tip for Moules Marinière, page 55.*

SEAFOOD WITH SPAGHETTI, CAPTAIN MORGAN

A delicious dish and so easy to prepare.

INGREDIENTS:

¼ cup olive oil
3 cloves garlic, minced
4 anchovy fillets, chopped
6 ounces calamari (squid), diced
1 pound ripe tomatoes, chopped
1 small green pepper, chopped
4 ounces medium-sized shrimp
4 ounces sea scallops
4 ounces baby clams, meat only
Pinch of crushed saffron
Salt to taste
Freshly ground pepper
12 ounces spaghetti, cooked for 7 to 10
   minutes
Freshly chopped parsley, for garnish

PREPARATION:

In a skillet, heat the oil and sauté the garlic; add anchovies, calamari, tomatoes and pepper. Cook for 40 minutes adding water if needed.

Add shrimp, scallops, clams and seasonings. Cook for 15 more minutes. Stir in the cooked and drained spaghetti.

To serve, transfer to a large serving bowl and sprinkle with freshly chopped parsley.

4 Servings.

VERMICELLI WITH SHRIMP IN CURRIED YOGURT

A wispy thin spaghetti, vermicelli is sometimes called angel hair pasta.

INGREDIENTS:

12 ounces vermicelli
4 tablespoons vegetable oil
1 small fresh hot chili pepper, finely minced
1 red sweet pepper, chopped
4 scallions, thinly sliced
8 ounces cooked bay shrimp, shelled and
   deveined
1 cup plain yogurt
¼ cup canned cream of coconut
2 tablespoons lemon juice
2 to 3 tablespoons curry powder
2 cloves garlic, minced
2 teaspoons minced fresh ginger
Salt
Freshly ground black pepper
1 mango, sliced
Unsweetened grated coconut
Peanuts and mint leaves for garnish

PREPARATION:

Cook the pasta in a gallon of boiling water with oil for 7 to 10 minutes. Drain and rinse well in cold water, then drain again. Transfer the cooked pasta to a large serving bowl and allow it to cool to room temperature, stirring occasionally to keep the pasta from sticking together.

Add chili pepper, sweet pepper, onions and shrimps to pasta and mix well.

To make the curry sauce, combine yogurt, cream of coconut, lemon juice, curry powder, garlic, ginger, salt and pepper to taste and mix it with the pasta.

Garnish the pasta with a sliced mango, grated coconut, peanuts and mint leaves.

6 to 8 Servings, as main course.
10 to 12 Servings, as side dish.

FETTUCINE MONTE CARLO 33

Smoked salmon in sauce over noodles — just right for a brunch or light luncheon entrée.

INGREDIENTS:

1 pound fettucine
1 cup heavy cream
6 tablespoons sweet butter
Scant pinch of freshly grated nutmeg
Salt and freshly ground black pepper
2 tablespoons chopped parsley
4 tablespoons grated Parmesan cheese
1 cup smoked salmon, julienne cut

PREPARATION:

Cook the fettucine in boiling salted water for about 7 minutes or until it is *al dente*.

While the fettucine is cooking, heat the cream, butter, nutmeg, salt and pepper in a large pan over low heat. Whisk the mixture constantly for 1 minute. Add the parsley.

Drain the noodles and add them to the sauce in the pan. Sprinkle with the grated cheese, add the smoked salmon and toss quickly to coat all the noodles.

Serve immediately with additional grated Parmesan cheese and black pepper.

6 Servings.

Fettucine Monte Carlo.

GNOCCHI ALLA ROMANA

(SEMOLINA DUMPLINGS)

An enduring favorite in Italian cookery, gnocchi, *or "little dumplings," originated in Rome many years ago. Over the years many varieties have evolved.*

INGREDIENTS:

3 cups milk
1½ teaspoons salt
Pinch of ground nutmeg
Freshly ground pepper
1 cup semolina or cream of wheat
2 eggs
½ cup grated Parmesan cheese
6 tablespoons butter or margarine, melted

PREPARATION:

Butter a large baking sheet and set it aside.

In a heavy 2- to 3-quart saucepan over moderate heat, bring the milk to a boil. Add salt, nutmeg and a few grains of pepper, and stir in the semolina with a wooden spoon. Cook and stir for 15 minutes, or until the semolina is so thick the spoon will stand up alone in the middle of the pan. Remove the pan from the heat.

Beat the eggs lightly with a fork, add ¼ cup of the cheese and stir the mixture into the semolina. Blend well and spoon the mixture onto the buttered baking sheet. Using a spatula, spread the batter into a sheet about ¾-inch thick. Refrigerate it for at least an hour, or until it is firm.

Preheat the oven to 400 degrees and butter an 8- or 9-inch baking dish. With a 1½-inch cookie cutter, cut as many discs as possible. (Or cut it into triangles with a sharp knife.) Place the remaining part of the mixture in the center of the baking dish and cover it with the discs. Sprinkle the top with melted butter and grated cheese.

Bake the gnocchi for 25 minutes, or until they are crisp and lightly golden. If you want to brown them, put them under a hot broiler for 30 seconds. They should be served at once while they are still bubbling from the heat of the oven.

4 Servings.

POTATO GNOCCHI

One of the most frequently ordered dishes.

INGREDIENTS:

4 (6 to 8 ounces, each) russet potatoes, cooked in skins and peeled
3 egg yolks, or 1 whole egg only
2 cups plus 2 tablespoons, all-purpose flour
Salt to taste

PREPARATION:

Mash the potatoes while they are warm. Add egg and flour and mix well to make a medium-soft dough. Form the dough into a ball, cover with a napkin or plastic wrap, and set it aside for 15 minutes.

Cut the dough into 10 small pieces and shape each piece into a rope (similar to a bread stick). Line up 2 at a time and sprinkle them with flour. Cut into 1-inch pieces. With a fork, indent the center of each gnocchi and roll them.

Drop the gnocchi into 1 gallon of boiling salted water. Allow them to rise to the top of the water, and simmer for 3 minutes.

Drain and serve them with pesto, meat or tomato sauce.

4 Servings.

SPAGHETTI AGLIO E OLIO

This is a flavorful example of a simple pasta dish.

INGREDIENTS:

**1 pound spaghetti
⅓ cup olive oil
4 cloves garlic, crushed
3 tablespoons fresh Italian (flat leaf) parsley, minced
4 tablespoons freshly grated Parmesan cheese
Salt and pepper**

PREPARATION:

In a gallon of boiling water, cook the spaghetti *al dente* (for 7 to 10 minutes). Drain well.

In a large skillet, heat the oil and brown the garlic in it. Discard the garlic, then add the drained spaghetti to the skillet and toss; heat for 1 minute. Toss with parsley. Before serving, add Parmesan cheese and freshly ground pepper.

4 Servings.

SPAGHETTI SCARPARA (SHOEMAKER)

This recipe serves two, because it is the original one invented by Pasquale Aventurato, who was a poor, but happy, Neapolitan shoemaker who used to make the spaghetti this way for his wife — long before women's lib.

INGREDIENTS:

**7 ounces spaghetti
3 tablespoons olive oil
2 cloves of garlic, crushed
5 ripe plum tomatoes, chopped
5 fresh basil leaves
Salt
⅛ teaspoon freshly ground pepper
Pinch of fresh oregano
1 tablespoon chopped parsley**

PREPARATION:

In a deep pot, cook the spaghetti *al dente* (for about 7 minutes) in boiling salted water.

In a medium-sized skillet, heat the oil and sauté the garlic until golden brown, add the tomatoes, basil leaves, salt, pepper, and oregano.

Cook for 7 to 10 minutes at high heat, stirring occasionally.

Drain the spaghetti well. Combine the spaghetti with the sauce and sauté for 2 minutes.

Serve on 2 dinner plates and sprinkle with parsley.

2 Servings.

36

PARTY GOURMET SPAGHETTI

The liquor in this recipe will affect the flavor. Vodka, for instance, gives it a creamy flavor — rather like carbonara.

TOMATO SAUCE:

INGREDIENTS:

½ pound plum tomatoes, cut in halves
2 cloves garlic, crushed
1 small carrot, cut up
1 small onion, quartered
¼ cup fresh basil leaves
¼ cup Italian parsley
4 tablespoons butter or olive oil
Salt and pepper
Dash each of oregano, marjoram, thyme and nutmeg
8 ounces water

PREPARATION:

In a large saucepan, combine all the ingredients. Cover and bring to a boil. Reduce the heat and simmer slowly for 1½ hours, stirring occasionally. Strain through a sieve or vegetable mill.

GOURMET SPAGHETTI:

INGREDIENTS:

3 tablespoons butter
1 cup Tomato Sauce
12 ounces spaghetti, cooked 7 to 10 minutes, and drained
⅓ cup heavy cream
2 egg yolks
Dash nutmeg
3 ounces of alternatively, vodka, cognac, or Scotch whiskey or, 5 ounces champagne
½ teaspoon salt
5 tablespoons grated Parmesan cheese
Freshly ground pepper to taste

PREPARATION:

In a large skillet, melt butter, add the tomato sauce and stir for 1 minute. Stir in the spaghetti.

In a separate skillet, mix together cream, egg yolks, nutmeg and one of the liquors or champagne. Add the pasta mixed with the tomato sauce, and heat it for a few minutes. Finally, sprinkle the top with Parmesan cheese; add freshly ground pepper to taste and serve.

Serves 4.

Fusilli or Pasta Primavera.

FUSILLI OR PASTA PRIMAVERA

Fusilli is the long, spiral-shaped pasta that resembles corkscrew curls. It is considered a good choice because the curls hold the sauce well.

INGREDIENTS:

12 ounces fusilli or other type of pasta
¼ cup (4 tablespoons) butter or margarine
3 cloves garlic, finely chopped
1 cup broccoli flowerets
1 small zucchini, julienne
1 yellow crookneck squash, julienne
1 small leek, the white part only, julienne
½ cup sliced mushrooms
1 small carrot, julienne
Juice of 1 lemon
1 cup water
Salt and pepper to taste
½ cup heavy cream
¼ cup (4 tablespoons) grated Parmesan
  cheese

PREPARATION:

Cook the pasta in boiling salted water for about 7 minutes, or *al dente*.

In a large skillet, melt the butter and sauté the garlic. Add all the vegetables, lemon juice, water, salt and pepper. Cook until the water evaporates and the vegetables are tender.

Add the precooked pasta and sauté with the vegetables. Finally, add cream and sprinkle with grated Parmesan cheese.

4 Servings.

PENNE PROVENÇALE SALAD

Eggplant salad with roasted peppers. The various ingredients for this salad are prepared separately and then mixed together. It is a welcome addition to a buffet table or an outdoor barbecue.

INGREDIENTS:

1 medium-sized eggplant, unpeeled and cut into 1-inch cubes
1 cup olive oil
Salt
1 medium-sized onion, sliced
2 red, sweet peppers, thinly sliced
2 cloves garlic, finely minced or pressed
Salt and freshly ground black pepper
2 tablespoons lemon juice
2 teaspoons dried herbes de Provence
12 ounces penne* (quill-shaped tubes)
½ cup chopped fresh basil

PREPARATION:

Preheat the oven to 400 degrees.

Place the eggplant cubes in a shallow baking pan, toss with ½ cup of the olive oil and sprinkle with salt. Bake the eggplant cubes until they are soft but still hold their shape, about 30 minutes. Set aside to cool.

Heat ¼ cup of the olive oil in a large, heavy skillet. Add onion slices and sweet peppers and cook over very low heat until the vegetables are quite tender and slightly caramelized, about

35 to 45 minutes. Stir in garlic, salt and pepper to taste and cook for 5 minutes longer.

Combine the remaining ¼ cup olive oil, lemon juice and herbes de Provence. Add salt and pepper, if you like. Whisk the mixture and reserve.

Cook the pasta in boiling water until *al dente*. Drain and rinse well in cold water, then drain again.

Toss the pasta in a salad bowl with the onion and peppers and the reserved dressing.

Gently stir in the eggplant cubes and chopped basil. Garnish with basil leaves.

PENNE ALLA CARBONARA

As the story goes, outdoor workers, such as wood-cutters, carried with them the ingredients for this luncheon dish, because they were easy to carry and cook.

INGREDIENTS:

1 pound penne*
4 egg yolks
½ cup heavy cream
4 tablespoons grated Romano or Parmesan cheese
Freshly ground pepper and salt
1 small onion, chopped
6 ounces pancetta (salted pork belly) or bacon, cut in julienne strips
4 tablespoons butter

---

* **Note:** *Penne (pronounced "pen-ay") is a pasta that is made in the shape of a quill or pen and is available in specialty food shops and Italian grocery stores.*

PREPARATION:

Cook the penne in boiling salted water for 12 minutes until *al dente* — as package directs.

In a small bowl, beat together the egg yolks, cream, cheese, pepper and just a pinch of salt.

In a large skillet, sauté the onion and bacon until it is slightly crispy. Drain off the fat. Pour the water off the pasta and mix together pasta, onion, bacon and soft butter. Stir and cook briefly over low heat. Add the egg mixture, tossing to coat pasta. Do not overcook. Serve creamy.

4 Servings.

BAKED MACARONI WITH RICOTTA

A variation on the macaroni and cheese theme with the addition of eggplant.

INGREDIENTS:

½ cup olive oil
1 large eggplant, peeled and diced ½-inch thick
2 tablespoons all-purpose flour
12 ounces elbow macaroni, cooked 7 to 10 minutes and drained
1 cup Fresh Tomato Sauce (see page 77)
½ cup grated Romano cheese
Salt and freshly ground pepper
½ cup ricotta cheese
3 tablespoons butter or margarine, melted

PREPARATION:

Preheat the oven to 400 degrees.

In a large skillet, heat the oil. Sprinkle diced eggplant with flour and sauté until all the pieces are brown, then drain. Toss drained macaroni with Tomato Sauce, grated cheese and freshly ground pepper. Add eggplant and ricotta. Salt to taste.

Pour the macaroni mixture into a buttered casserole. Pour butter over the top, and bake for about 15 minutes, or until the top of the macaroni and cheese is firm and golden brown.

4 Servings.

40

TAGLIATELLE WITH WALNUT SAUCE

Tagliatelle are long, narrow noodles that are a specialty of Bologna. There, proudly displayed in a sealed glass case at the chamber of commerce is a solid-gold noodle, one millimeter thick and six millimeters wide — the standard dimensions for the perfect raw tagliatelle noodle.

INGREDIENTS:

1 pound Tagliatelle (fresh noodles)
2 tablespoons olive oil
1 small onion, chopped
½ cup shelled walnuts
6 ounces ricotta cheese
2 ounces heavy cream
2 tablespoons butter
¾ teaspoon salt
Freshly ground pepper to taste
Dash each of nutmeg, clove and marjoram
10 sprigs Italian parsley
¼ cup walnut halves
4 tablespoons grated Parmesan cheese

PREPARATION:

Cook the Tagliatelle in a gallon of boiling salted water for about 7 minutes, or *al dente*.

While the noodles are cooking, sauté the onion with oil for 2 minutes at medium heat.

In a food processor fitted with a metal chopping blade, place ½ cup of the walnuts, ricotta, cream, butter, fried onion, salt, pepper, seasoning and parsley. Chop the ingredients until you have a smooth mixture.

Drain the pasta, leaving it slightly wet. Transfer to a serving bowl and pour the walnut sauce over it. Toss gently and serve topped with walnut halves and grated cheese.

6 to 8 Servings.

Opposite page: Paella Valenciana, recipe on page 52.

SEAFOOD

42

Sole Fillets Amandine
Tuna Peppersteak
Kingfish Suprême Buccaneer
Salmon Suprême in Ginger Soya Sauce
Sea Bass al Cartoccio
Halibut Steaks with Piquant Sauce
Red Snapper Louisiana
Koftas
Bouillabaisse
Maracaibo Fish Pepperpot
Jambalaya aux Crevettes
Sitka Fish Stew
Cacciuco Livornese
Paella Valenciana
Au Gratin Sea Scallops Calypso
Moules Marinière
King Crabmeat Newburg
Scampi Flambé with Anisette
Garlic Shrimp

Sole Fillets Amandine, recipe on opposite page.

SOLE FILLETS AMANDINE

This is the classic method of preparing sautéed fish fillets. Serve the fillets with potatoes and Dutch Cucumber Salad (see page 95).

INGREDIENTS:

8 (4-ounce) sole fillets
1 tablespoon all-purpose flour
6 tablespoons butter or margarine
Salt and pepper
⅓ cup blanched almonds, sliced
3 tablespoons lemon juice
2 tablespoons chopped parsley

PREPARATION:

Sprinkle the sole with flour and sauté quickly in the butter. Turn once, season and cook until the fish is golden and crisp; remove the fillets from the pan and place them on a warmed serving dish.

Sauté the almonds in the remaining butter in the pan. Add lemon juice and chopped parsley and pour the sauce over the sole.

4 Servings.

TUNA PEPPERSTEAK

43

A very good, savory method of preparation for any fish steaks — thick crosscuts of larger fish like swordfish, red snapper, halibut, salmon and tuna.

INGREDIENTS:

4 tuna steaks, about ½ pound each and
   ½-inch thick
Juice of 1 lemon
2 tablespoons olive oil
4 teaspoons freshly ground green pepper
½ teaspoon salt
3 tablespoons butter or margarine
1 bay leaf
2 cloves
1 tablespoon capers, washed and drained
1 tablespoon Worcestershire sauce
3 tablespoons fresh parsley, finely chopped

PREPARATION:

Marinate the tuna for 1 hour in the combined lemon juice, olive oil, pepper and salt.

In a small, 7-inch skillet, melt the butter; add bay leaf, cloves and capers. Cook until the butter turns dark brown; add the Worcestershire sauce and remove the pan from the heat.

Warm the broiler; cook steaks for 5 minutes. Turn them over and cook another for 5 minutes. Place cooked steaks on a serving platter. Pour sauce which has been heated back up to a boil over the top of the steak. Garnish with chopped parsley and serve.

4 Servings.

44

KINGFISH SUPRÊME BUCCANEER

Fit for a king.

INGREDIENTS:

¼ cup olive oil
1 small red onion, julienne
½ pound ripe tomatoes, chopped
1 green pepper, julienne
4 ounces dry white wine
½ teaspoon oregano
½ teaspoon thyme
Tabasco sauce to taste
4 cups Fish Fumet (see page 52)
4 (7-ounce) fresh kingfish fillets

PREPARATION:

In a skillet, sauté the onion in olive oil until it is transparent. Add the next 6 ingredients; bring to a boil. Reduce heat; simmer for 30 minutes, stirring occasionally.

In a separate skillet or sauté pan, poach the fish with 1 quart of Fish Fumet. Cook slowly for 30 minutes.

Place each fish fillet in an individual serving dish and cover each with a generous quantity of sauce.

CHEF'S TIP:

Kingfish is a Florida fish. If it is unavailable in your area, substitute bass or white fish. Two cups of the Fish Fumet can be replaced by 2 cups of white wine.

4 Servings.

SALMON SUPRÊME IN GINGER SOYA SAUCE

This has an excellent, delicate flavor, and is relatively fast to prepare.

INGREDIENTS:

1 tablespoon cornstarch
2 tablespoons all-purpose flour
4 (8-ounce) fresh salmon fillets
¼ cup (4 tablespoons) butter
2 tablespoons honey
2 ounces fresh ginger root, chopped, or
    ½ teaspoon powdered ginger
3 tablespoons soya sauce
½ teaspoon garlic powder
1 tablespoon balsamic vinegar
3 ounces dry sherry
2 scallions, chopped

PREPARATION:

Combine cornstarch and flour and sprinkle it on both sides of the salmon slices. In a skillet, melt the butter and sauté the salmon at medium heat for a total of 15 minutes.

Transfer the cooked salmon to a warm serving dish. To the fat remaining in the skillet, add honey, ginger, soya sauce, garlic powder, vinegar, sherry and scallions. Bring the mixture just to a boil, and pour it over the fish before serving.

4 Servings.

Sea Bass Al Cartoccio.

SEA BASS AL CARTOCCIO

A salt water fish, sea bass is a member of the grouper family. Its texture and flavor resemble striped bass. These cartoccio *("paper bags") absorb the flavor of the sauce beautifully, and each diner opens a bag, releasing an appetizing aroma.*

INGREDIENTS:

2 pounds sea bass, cut in small cubes and marinated in salt, pepper, lemon juice and olive oil for 2 hours.
3 cloves garlic, minced
2 tablespoons fresh parsley, chopped
1 rib celery, chopped
1 teaspoon capers, chopped
12 Kalamata (Greek) olives
1½ pounds ripe tomatoes, chopped
6 ounces dry white wine
4 tablespoons olive oil
½ teaspoon oregano
4 fresh basil leaves
4 sheets aluminum foil
Salt and pepper to taste

PREPARATION:

In a mixing bowl, combine garlic, parsley, celery, capers, olives, tomatoes, wine, olive oil, oregano and basil leaves. This mixture should have a sour taste, and should not be cooked.

Divide the marinated fish into 4 equal portions. Place each portion in the center of the aluminum foil and cover with uncooked sauce. Wrap the fish in foil and seal the edges.

Place the packages of fish in a baking pan and bake for 35 minutes.

Serve in their bags and accompany with garlic toast.

4 Servings.

HALIBUT STEAKS WITH PIQUANT SAUCE

The mild-flavored halibut benefits from marinating.

INGREDIENTS:

4 halibut steaks (8 ounce), ¾-inch thick
4 tablespoons olive oil
2 tablespoons fresh lemon juice
Freshly ground pepper
4 fresh oregano sprigs
1 cup Piquant Sauce

PREPARATION:

Place the fish in a dish large enough to accommodate it in a single layer. Drizzle with oil and lemon juice, and sprinkle with pepper. Turn to coat both sides. Scatter oregano sprigs over the fish. Cover and allow it to marinate for 30 minutes, refrigerated.

Preheat the broiler. Place the marinated fillets on a greased rack and cook to desired doneness, about 5 minutes per side.

Transfer the fish to a serving platter. Top with Piquant Sauce and serve with steamed rice.

4 Servings.

PIQUANT SAUCE:

INGREDIENTS:

⅓ cup olive oil
⅓ cup minced fresh Italian parsley
⅓ cup pickled red bell pepper strips, drained and diced
⅓ cup thinly sliced green onion
2 tablespoons fresh lemon juice
1 teaspoon minced fresh oregano
2 teaspoons capers, drained and rinsed

PREPARATION:

Combine oil, parsley, bell pepper strips, onions, lemon juice, oregano and capers in a medium-sized, heavy saucepan over low heat. Cook 5 minutes to blend flavors, stirring occasionally. Taste, adding more lemon juice and capers if desired.

Makes about 1 cup.

RED SNAPPER LOUISIANA

This is a beautiful fish from the Gulf of Mexico — an all-time favorite.

INGREDIENTS:

1½ pounds red snapper
2 tablespoons unsalted butter
⅓ cup dry white wine
⅔ cup heavy cream
1 teaspoon Dijon mustard
Salt
½ teaspoon freshly ground white pepper
2 tablespoons chopped fresh parsley
1 tablespoon mustard seed

PREPARATION:

In a large skillet, over medium heat, sauté the fish in butter for about 5 minutes. Remove to a warm plate with slotted spoon. Cover and keep fish warm.

Add wine to the skillet. Cook the wine and accumulated juices from the fish over high heat until the wine is reduced by half. Add cream and cook over medium heat until the sauce is reduced and thick. Swirl in mustard. Taste and adjust seasonings if necessary.

Spoon sauce over the snapper. Garnish with chopped parsley and mustard seed, and serve.

4 Servings.

KOFTAS

(INDIAN FISH BALLS)

A succulent Indian way with fish.

INGREDIENTS:

**1 pound white meat fish, poached and
　shredded
1 small onion, chopped
2 cloves garlic, minced
3 tablespoons mango pulp
2 tablespoons dairy sour cream
½ teaspoon chili powder
½ teaspoon turmeric
1 teaspoon curry powder
2 eggs beaten
1½ cups bread crumbs
Salt to taste
½ cup soy or olive oil**

PREPARATION:

In a large saucepan or fish poacher, simmer liquid (water or milk) and poach fish. Place flaked fish in a medium-sized bowl; discard skin and bones. Stir in onion, garlic, mango pulp, sour cream, and spices. Refrigerate the mixture for about an hour to make it easier to shape the balls.

With your hands, make small balls out of the fish mixture. Dip and coat each one in the egg mixture, roll it in bread crumbs spread on waxed paper.

In a deep saucepan, heat the oil to 375 degrees. Add the fish balls a few at a time and fry until golden. Drain on paper towels.

Serve with curried rice and garnish with lemon slices.

CHEF'S TIP:

To make mango pulp: Peel the skin of a small mango and slice the pulp from the seed lengthwise.

4 Servings.

48

Bouillabaisse.

BOUILLABAISSE

(MEDITERRANEAN SEAFOOD STEW)

The distinguishing feature of a bouillabaisse *from other fish stews is the seasonings—saffron, garlic, tomatoes, onion and herbs native to Provençe, in southern France. Except for the seasonings, you may make substitutions, according to the fish available.*

FISH STOCK:

INGREDIENTS:

1 pound fish heads, cut in half
2 medium-sized ripe tomatoes, quartered
4 cloves garlic, crushed
1 small onion, sliced
4 tablespoons olive oil
1 bay leaf
Bouquet garni (fresh fennel, parsley, thyme)
½ teaspoon saffron
Peel of half an orange
2½ pints water
6 ounces dry white wine

PREPARATION:

In a large saucepan, combine fish heads, tomatoes, garlic, onion, oil, bay leaf, bouquet garni, saffron and orange peel, water and wine. Cover and bring to a boil and cook slowly for 30 minutes. At this point, liquid will be reduced by half and the fish stock is ready to be strained.

Makes about 3 cups of stock.

STEW:

INGREDIENTS:

6 ounces ocean perch, cut into 1-inch pieces
6 ounces John Dory or sole, cut into 1-inch pieces
6 ounces conger eel, cut into 1-inch pieces
6 ounces sea bass, cut into 1-inch pieces
12 jumbo shrimp, peeled and deveined
8 soft shell crabs or crab leg equivalent
Salt to taste
Dash of Tabasco sauce
2 tablespoons parsley, chopped
1 loaf French bread, sliced and toasted

PREPARATION:

Pour strained fish stock into a skillet and add conger eel and sea bass; cook for 10 minutes. Add perch, John Dory, crab and shrimp; cook for 5 more minutes. Add a dash of Tabasco sauce and sprinkle with parsley and salt to taste.

Line a soup tureen or a large bowl with sliced and toasted French bread. Add the fish and pour the stock over the top.

To serve, ladle the *Bouillabaisse* into soup bowls and pass the rest of the bread for dunking.

CHEF'S TIP:

Timing is important in preparing *Bouillabaisse;* those fish that need less cooking time are added last. The taste and the texture of each fish should come through, but they should not be overcooked.

4 Servings.

50

MARACAIBO FISH PEPPERPOT

This recipe gets its name from the city of Maracaibo, located in Venezuela at Lake Maracaibo's outlet to the Caribbean Sea.

INGREDIENTS:

2 tablespoons olive or corn oil
1 small red onion, chopped
1 rib celery, chopped
1 clove garlic, crushed
3½ cups water
½ pound red snapper, skinned, boned, cut in
   1-inch cubes
1 large red pepper, minced
1 teaspoon orange peel, minced
1 ripe tomato, chopped
1 teaspoon mace powder
Salt and pepper to taste
¼ teaspoon Tabasco sauce
4 tablespoons steamed rice

PREPARATION:

In a large pot, warm the oil and combine onion, celery and garlic; stir until they are transparent. Add water, fish and all other ingredients except the steamed rice. Bring to a boil, reduce heat and simmer slowly for 1 hour.

To serve, ladle the stew into soup bowls, and top with 1 tablespoon of steamed rice for each portion.

CHEF'S TIP:

Mahi Mahi is a good substitute when red snapper is unavailable.

4 Servings.

JAMBALAYA AUX CREVETTES

This Louisiana dish of Creole origin may be made with other seafood instead of shrimp, but to be "real" Jambalaya, rice is essential.

INGREDIENTS:

3 tablespoons butter
2 slices bacon, chopped
1 small onion, chopped
1 rib celery, chopped
1 green pepper, chopped
2 cloves garlic, minced
2 large ripe tomatoes, chopped
1 teaspoon chili powder
½ teaspoon Tabasco sauce
Pinch cayenne pepper
½ cup uncooked rice
2 cups chicken stock
1½ pounds raw shrimp, medium-sized,
   shelled and deveined
2 scallions, chopped
2 tablespoons parsley, chopped
Salt to taste

PREPARATION:

In a large saucepan, heat the butter and bacon; sauté the onion, celery, green pepper and garlic until they are soft. Add the remaining ingredients except the shrimp, scallions and parsley and cook for 10 minutes or until the rice is tender; stir occasionally. Add shrimp and cook for 15 more minutes. Finally, add the scallions and parsley; heat, stir and serve.

4 Servings.

SITKA FISH STEW

Just the thing for a cold winter evening.

INGREDIENTS:

1 medium onion, diced
½ cup diced leeks
½ cup diced celery
6 tablespoons butter or margarine
1 (8-ounce) bottle clam juice
1 cup dry white wine
2 garlic cloves
1 bay leaf
½ teaspoon thyme
¼ teaspoon freshly ground black pepper
Dash of Tabasco sauce
⅓ cup finely chopped fresh parsley
12 hard shell clams in shells, scrubbed
½ pound silver salmon, cut in small chunks
¾ pound halibut, cut in small chunks
12 large shrimp, peeled and deveined
1 cup Tomato Sauce (see page 36)

PREPARATION:

In a large kettle over medium heat, sauté onion, leeks and celery in butter until golden brown. Add clam juice, wine, garlic, bay leaf, thyme, black pepper, Tabasco sauce and parsley. Heat to boiling, then simmer uncovered for 5 minutes.

Add clams and simmer for 5 minutes. Add salmon and simmer for 3 minutes. Stir in halibut and shrimp and simmer for 3 minutes more or until clams are open and flesh barely separates when tested with dinner knife. Remove bay leaf. Stir in Tomato Sauce.

To serve, ladle soup into shallow bowls, arranging shrimp on top.

4 Servings.

CACCIUCO LIVORNESE

51

Cacciuco is a generic name for a fish casserole and this one is named after Livorno (Leghorn), one of Italy's busiest ports.

INGREDIENTS:

⅓ cup olive oil
1 medium-sized onion, chopped
1 rib celery, chopped
4 cloves garlic, chopped
2 bay leaves
2 pounds ripe tomatoes, peeled and chopped
2 cups dry white wine
2 cups Fish Fumet (see page 52)
2 pounds grouper or rock fish, cut in 12 pieces
1 pound shrimp, peeled and deveined
1 pound sea scallops
Salt and pepper to taste
Clams, mussels, garlic croutons* for garnish
3 tablespoons chopped parsley for garnish

PREPARATION:

In a flameproof casserole, heat the oil and sauté the onion and celery until they are transparent, then add garlic; fry 1 minute. Add bay leaves and tomato and cook for 20 minutes.

Add the wine, Fish Fumet and grouper, shrimp and sea scallops; cook for 25 to 30 minutes. Season to taste. Cacciuco is now ready to be served. You may garnish with clams, mussels, garlic croutons and sprinkle with chopped parsley.

---

* **Note:** *For instructions to make garlic croutons, see Caesar Salad recipe (see page 92).*

6 Servings.

52   PAELLA VALENCIANA

This Spanish mélange *is traditionally served in a* paelleron, *a wide, flat serving dish, with mussels and clams arranged on top. It makes a beautiful buffet dish. (See photograph on page 41.)*

INGREDIENTS:

¼ cup olive oil
1 medium-sized onion, chopped
3 cloves garlic, chopped
1 pound boneless chicken, cut in morsels
1 large tomato
1 pound Spanish rice
1½ cups Fish Fumet
6 ounces dry chorizo
½ teaspoon crushed saffron
½ cup fresh red pepper, chopped
½ cup fresh green peas
Pinch each of salt and freshly ground pepper
1 pound cooked lobster meat in small pieces
1 pound large shrimp, peeled and deveined
2 dozen mussels
1 dozen clams

PREPARATION:

In a 4-quart pot, heat the oil over medium heat; sauté the onion and garlic in the oil, then add chicken and stir. Let the chicken brown: add tomato and cook for 10 minutes. Add all remaining ingredients, except the seafood. Cover and simmer over low heat for 15 minutes. Add the shrimp. Cook for 10 minutes more. Then add the lobster and cook for 5 more minutes. The rice should be tender at that point.

In the meantime, in a large saucepan, steam the mussels and clams over high heat for 6 to 8 minutes (all the shells should be open). Rinse to get all traces of sand out.

When the rice is tender, add the clams and mussels to it.

6 Servings.

FISH FUMET:

INGREDIENTS:

1 pound assorted bony fish, or 1 fish head
1 rib celery
1 bunch parsley
1 cup dry white wine
1 quart water
Bouquet garni (assorted fresh herbs, i.e.
   thyme, marjoram, sage, rosemary, etc.)

PREPARATION:

Wash fish well and remove gills from the head. Combine all the ingredients in a large pot, and bring to a boil. Reduce the heat, and simmer for 20 minutes. Strain. Taste and add salt as needed. Any excess *fumet* can be frozen and used at some other time.

Makes about 4 cups.

AU GRATIN SEA SCALLOPS CALYPSO

This lively sauce gives a Caribbean flavor to sea scallops.

INGREDIENTS:

**2 tablespoons olive oil
2 tablespoons chives, finely chopped
1 pound sea scallops
2 tablespoons rum
Dash of Tabasco sauce
Pinch each of ginger powder and paprika
3 tablespoons butter or margarine
3 tablespoons all-purpose flour
Salt and pepper to taste
½ cup milk, warmed
2 tablespoons grated Swiss cheese
1 tablespoon parsley, finely chopped**

PREPARATION:

Preheat the oven to 450 degrees.

In a large skillet over medium heat, sauté the chives for 2 minutes. Raise heat to high; add sea scallops and cook for another 2 minutes. Then add rum, Tabasco sauce, ginger powder and paprika; continue cooking for 2 minutes. Remove from heat.

In a 2-quart saucepan, melt the butter; blend in flour, salt and pepper. Add warm milk all at once; cook quickly, stirring constantly, until mixture bubbles and thickens (3 to 4 minutes). Add Swiss cheese; stir until melted. Mix the sauce with the sea scallops.

Au Gratin Sea Scallops Calypso.

Transfer the mixture to a medium-sized baking dish, or 4 individual baking shells. Sprinkle with parsley. Bake at 450 degrees for 10 minutes.

4 Servings.

54

MOULES MARINIÈRE

(MUSSELS MARINARA)

These mussels in "sailor-style" sauce make a simple and savory meal. Serve extra French bread to soak up the sauce.

THE MUSSELS:

INGREDIENTS:

3 pounds (about 40) cleaned mussels
3 cloves garlic, crushed
3 tablespoons olive oil
1 cup Marinara Sauce
1 cup dry white wine
1 loaf French bread, sliced
4 tablespoons chopped parsley

PREPARATION:

In a large pot, sauté the garlic in oil until it is golden brown. Add the sauce, wine and mussels. Cover and cook the mussels over high heat, stirring occasionally, for 5 minutes, or until the mussels are open. Do not overcook; meat should be uniform and milky in color. Discard any mussels which are not open.

To serve, place a slice of French bread on the bottoms of individual soup bowls. Ladle the mussels, including shells, on top of the bread and spoon the Marinara Sauce over the mussels. Sprinkle with parsley.

CHEF'S TIP:

To clean mussels, use a small paring knife and scrape all the dirt off the shells. Cut or pull off the beard, and scrub the mussel shells under cold running water. Then let them soak an hour in cold salted water. Rinse once more.

Use green mussels if you can find them, but they are not easily available in the United States.

4 Servings.

MARINARA SAUCE:

INGREDIENTS:

4 tablespoons olive oil
1 onion, chopped
1 carrot, chopped
1 rib celery, sliced
2 pounds ripe plum tomatoes, quartered
¼ cup parsley
¼ teaspoon dried hot pepper
2 garlic cloves, minced
¼ teaspoon salt

PREPARATION:

Heat the olive oil in a saucepan and sauté the onion, carrot and celery until the onion is soft. Add all other ingredients. Stir and cook uncovered for 30 minutes at medium heat. Strain the sauce through a food mill or a sieve.

Makes 2 cups.

Opposite page: Moules Marinière.

KING CRABMEAT NEWBURG

The spicy sauce works well with the delicate flavor of the crabmeat. A new twist on an old favorite, the almonds give this luxuriously creamy sauce the crunch it needs.

INGREDIENTS:

2 tablespoons butter
2 tablespoons all-purpose flour
⅓ cup heavy cream
½ cup sour cream
Juice of 1 lemon
1 pound crabmeat, cooked and diced
1 tablespoon freshly chopped parsley
⅓ cup almonds, blanched, skinned and sliced
¼ teaspoon Worcestershire sauce
Dash of nutmeg
Dash of Tabasco sauce

PREPARATION:

In a 2-quart saucepan, make a *roux*: Melt the butter; blend in the flour thoroughly. Add cream and sour cream; reduce heat to low. Stir constantly, simmering until the mixture thickens. Add the remaining ingredients. Gently simmer for 10 minutes; serve over hot cooked rice.

6 Servings.

SCAMPI FLAMBÉ WITH ANISETTE

A dramatic way to serve scampi.

INGREDIENTS:

¼ cup (4 tablespoons) butter
1 tablespoon olive oil
1 leek, chopped, white part only
2 pounds large shrimp (15 to 18 per pound),
    peeled and deveined
⅓ cup fresh basil leaves
1 cup fresh anise leaves
1 teaspoon Italian herbs
3 ounces anisette liqueur
2 ounces brandy
Salt and freshly ground pepper to taste
Risotto alla Milanese (see page 30)

PREPARATION:

In a large skillet with butter and oil, sauté the leek until golden brown. Add scampi, stir for 2 minutes. Add basil, anise leaves and Italian herbs; stir and cook for 3 more minutes.

Pour in anisette and brandy. Add seasonings. Adjust to high heat to flame. Serve over Risotto alla Milanese.

4 Servings.

Opposite page: Scampi Flambé with Anisette.

58 GARLIC SHRIMP

Shrimp made this way are an easy, quick dish for a party. Serve with basil fettucine, or other herbed pastas. (See photograph on the front cover.)

INGREDIENTS:

10 cloves garlic, finely minced
2 tablespoons olive oil
1 cup dry white wine
4 whole cloves
1½ pounds large shrimp, peeled and deveined
1 teaspoon Dijon mustard
Salt and pepper to taste
½ teaspoon Worcestershire sauce
2 tablespoons chopped parsley
2 fresh bay leaves
2 cups cooked pasta or 4 slices bread
3 tablespoons butter
¼ cup grated Parmesan cheese

PREPARATION:

Preheat the oven to 400 degrees.

In a large skillet, brown ¾ of the garlic in oil; add wine, cloves and bay leaves. Cook slowly until the wine reduces to ⅔ of the original volume.

Add the shrimp, mustard, salt, pepper and Worcestershire sauce to the garlic/wine mixture. Cook for 3 or 4 minutes, just until the shrimp are tender. Sprinkle parsley over the top.

Fork pasta onto 4 individual plates. Transfer the shrimp onto the pasta and pour the remaining garlic/wine mixture over the shrimp.

If you wish, you can serve this shrimp with garlic bread triangles.

To make Garlic Bread Triangles: Spread the bread slices with butter that has been mixed with the remaining garlic and cheese. Place them in a baking pan and bake until the cheese is melted. Cut each slice of the bread into 4 triangles and serve.

4 Servings.

Opposite page: Canard Flambé aux Abricots (Flaming Duckling with Apricots), recipe on page 70.

POULTRY

60

Breast of Chicken Cordon Bleu
Southern Fried Chicken
Chicken à la King
Peking-Style Chicken in Mustard Sauce
Port of Spain Chicken
Chicken Cacciatora
Capon au Chambertin
Coq au Vin
Pheasant in Salmìs
Lime Broiled Squab
Roast Duckling with Pineapple Sauce
Canard Flambé aux Abricots

Breast of Chicken Cordon Bleu, recipe on opposite page.

BREAST OF CHICKEN CORDON BLEU

This stuffed chicken is a good choice when you have invited guests to dinner, because it can be prepared in advance.

INGREDIENTS:

2 egg whites
½ teaspoon nutmeg
½ teaspoon paprika
Salt and pepper
½ cup plain bread crumbs
2 tablespoons grated Parmesan cheese
4 skinned chicken breast halves, 6 ounces
  each
4 slices ham
4 slices Swiss cheese
4 tablespoons butter

PREPARATION:

Preheat the oven to 375 degrees.

In a large bowl, whisk the egg whites with nutmeg, paprika, salt and pepper until they are foamy. In another flat bowl, combine the bread crumbs and Parmesan cheese.

With a knife, open the chicken breasts and slice into the side of each one to make an inside pocket. Stuff each chicken breast with 1 slice of Swiss cheese and 1 slice of ham.

Dip the breast into the egg mixture, drain and place it in the bread crumb mixture. With the edge of the knife, pat the crumbs into each side of the chicken breasts.

In a large skillet, warm the butter and sauté the chicken for 3 minutes on each side. Place the chicken in a baking dish and bake in the oven for 15 more minutes.

4 Servings.

SOUTHERN FRIED CHICKEN

61

An American heritage recipe.

INGREDIENTS:

1 (2½-pound) fryer
4 tablespoons all-purpose flour
2 eggs, beaten
½ cup milk
1 teaspoon herbs (thyme, marjoram)
1 teaspoon salt
1 teaspoon freshly ground pepper
1½ cups bread crumbs
1 cup corn oil

PREPARATION:

Debone the chicken and cut it into 12 pieces. Rinse under cold water and pat dry. Sprinkle each piece with flour and dip it into eggs beaten with milk, herbs, salt and pepper. Roll the chicken pieces in bread crumbs.

In a large skillet, over high heat, heat the oil and fry the chicken, about 3 minutes on each side. Reduce the heat to medium, and cook, partially covered, for 35 to 40 minutes, turning the pieces occasionally, until they are done and golden brown. The juices of the chicken should run clear.

Drain the fried chicken on paper towels. Serve hot with cream gravy or cold with mustard and pickles.

4 Servings.

62

CHICKEN À LA KING

An American luncheon specialty. This creamed chicken dish is very good if it is served immediately after it is prepared.

INGREDIENTS:

1 small green pepper, chopped
½ pound fresh mushrooms, sliced
½ cup butter or margarine
½ cup all-purpose flour
2 cups milk
1 cup chicken stock
2 cups cooked, chopped chicken breast
1 (2-ounce) jar diced pimiento, drained
2 cups hot, cooked rice
4 patty shells

PREPARATION:

Cook and stir green pepper and mushrooms with butter or margarine in a saucepan over medium heat for 5 minutes. Stir in flour and make a *roux*, stirring constantly for 2 more minutes. Gradually add milk and 1 cup of chicken stock. Stir in chicken and pimiento and cook for 3 minutes, or until thoroughly heated.

Serve at once over rice or fill patty shells.

4 Servings.

PEKING-STYLE CHICKEN IN MUSTARD SAUCE

A pungent oriental sauce coats this crisp chicken to perfection.

INGREDIENTS:

½ cup soy oil (vegetable oil)
2 chicken breasts, boned and shredded
¼ cup cornstarch
3 egg whites, beaten
2 tablespoons sesame oil
3 tablespoons granulated sugar
2 tablespoons white vinegar
2 tablespoons soy sauce
1 tablespoon powdered mustard

PREPARATION:

Warm oil in a skillet or wok. Slice chicken into strips (2-inch by ⅓-inch), coat with cornstarch, then dip in egg whites. Sauté the chicken until it is crispy and brown.

To make the sauce: In a bowl, combine sesame oil, sugar, vinegar, soy sauce and mustard; blend thoroughly. Drain oil from the skillet, add sauce and cook for 5 minutes at low heat.

Serve over Chinese noodles or steamed rice.

4 Servings.

63

Peking-Style Chicken in Mustard Sauce.

64

PORT OF SPAIN CHICKEN

When it comes to cooking poultry, Creole cuisine is outstanding. This recipe has a tangy aroma and flavor.

INGREDIENTS:

2 tablespoons vegetable oil
¼ cup butter or margarine
4 slices bacon, chopped
1 (3½-pound) fryer, cut into serving pieces
2 tablespoons all-purpose flour
2 tablespoons mace
1 tablespoon finely chopped fresh ginger root
12 ounces orange juice

PREPARATION:

Heat oil, margarine and bacon over medium-high heat in a large casserole. Dust the chicken with flour and sauté on both sides for 10 minutes; remove excess grease with a spoon. Add mace, ginger and orange juice; reduce heat to medium-low and cook for 30 minutes or until juice is almost evaporated.

Serve with a first course of Chilled Gazpacho Soup (see page 26).

4 Servings.

CHICKEN CACCIATORA

Cacciatora, or "hunter's style" refers to any meat or fish cooked in a sauce that includes tomatoes, scallions, mushrooms, bay leaves and red or white wine.

INGREDIENTS:

1 (2-pound) fryer, cut up
¼ cup olive oil
½ cup chopped onion
3 garlic cloves, chopped
½ teaspoon oregano
Salt and freshly ground pepper
1 pound ripe plum tomatoes, chopped
½ cup dry red wine
½ pound mushrooms

PREPARATION:

Brown the chicken pieces in olive oil, then add onion, garlic and seasoning. Cook for about 5 minutes. Add tomatoes and wine. Cover and simmer for about 25 minutes or until chicken is tender. Add mushrooms and simmer for 15 more minutes before serving.

4 Servings.

Chicken Cacciatora.

Capon au Chambertin

65

Chambertin is a famous full-bodied burgundy wine, named after the French town where it originated. It was said to be Napoleon's favorite.

INGREDIENTS:

1 (5-pound) capon, cut into 12 pieces
2 tablespoons olive oil
4 tablespoons butter
4 shallots, minced
½ pound boleto mushrooms, cut in ½-inch pieces
2 cups Chambertin, or other dry red wine
3 ounces brandy
½ cup heavy cream
Pinch each of nutmeg and powdered clove
Salt and pepper to taste

PREPARATION:

Wash the capon pieces under cold water and pat dry.

In a large, heavy skillet or Dutch oven, melt oil and butter. Brown the capon pieces over medium-high heat on both sides. Add the shallots and stir for 1 or 2 minutes. Add mushrooms moistened with the Chambertin and brandy and simmer, tightly covered, for approximately 1 hour or until done. Add the cream and simmer for 2 more minutes.

Arrange the capon on a warm serving dish. Season the sauce and pour it over the capon.

4 Servings.

66 COQ AU VIN

We have inherited this classic recipe from the French. It is a favorite for buffet tables.

INGREDIENTS:

2 strips bacon, chopped
1 (2½-to 3-pound) fryer, cut up
Freshly ground pepper
6 shallots, chopped
2 garlic cloves, minced
¼ cup brandy
2 cups red burgundy wine
1 teaspoon granulated sugar
6 tablespoons butter or margarine
½ pound pearl onions
½ pound mushrooms, small size
Dash each of flour, nutmeg, salt and pepper
2 tablespoons fresh parsley, chopped

PREPARATION:

In a large skillet over moderate heat, fry the bacon pieces until crisp. Remove them with a slotted spoon and drain on paper towel.

Sprinkle the chicken pieces lightly with pepper. Brown the chicken in the drippings over moderate heat on both sides. Remove the chicken to a platter while you sauté the shallots and garlic for 5 minutes.

Return the chicken to the pan and heat it through. Remove from heat. Add the brandy and gently heat. (Be careful not to overheat.)

Turn off the heat. Light the brandy with a match and pour it flaming over the chicken as you shake the pan to spread it over the chicken until all the flames are extinguished.

Add the wine and sugar to the chicken. Bring to a boil over high heat, lower the heat and simmer, tightly covered, over low heat for about 25 minutes, or until the chicken is tender.

While the chicken is simmering, melt the butter in a heavy skillet over very low heat and sauté the onions very slowly. Cover and shake the pan frequently, so they cook evenly until they are tender but not browned. Remove them with a slotted spoon. Turn up the heat and sauté the mushrooms in the onion butter for a minute or two. Stir in the dash of flour, nutmeg, salt and pepper.

When the chicken is tender, skim the fat from the surface of the liquid and add the onions and mushrooms. Let the liquid simmer for another 5 minutes to heat through.

Garnish with parsley and bacon pieces before serving.

4 Servings.

Coq au Vin.

PHEASANT IN SALMÌS

68

In France, game birds are traditionally prepared in salmìs.

INGREDIENTS:

1 (2½-pound) pheasant, cleaned and cut up
    into 8 pieces (including the liver and heart)
2 cups red burgundy wine
1 rib celery, chopped
1 carrot, chopped
1 small onion, chopped
2 bay leaves
2 cloves garlic, crushed
6 peppercorns, crushed
Pinch of nutmeg
Pinch of sage
½ teaspoon salt
¼ teaspoon black pepper
1 leek, chopped, white part only
4 tablespoons butter
2 tablespoons all-purpose flour
¼ cup dairy sour cream

PREPARATION:

In a large bowl, combine the pheasant, liver, heart, wine, carrot, onion, bay leaves, peppercorns and herbs. Cover the bowl and marinate the pheasant in the refrigerator for at least 8 hours, turning occasionally.

Drain well, and reserve the marinade. Sprinkle the pheasant with flour.

In a large skillet, sauté the leek in butter. Brown the pheasant on all sides. Add the marinade, cover, reduce the heat and simmer slowly for 1½ hours.

Remove the pheasant pieces to an oven-proof serving platter. Place it in a warm oven. Pour the marinade through a sieve into a saucepan. Add the flour and sour cream; cook and stir over low heat to obtain a medium-thick sauce. Pour the sauce over the pheasant and serve with fresh noodles or wild rice.

4 Servings.

LIME BROILED SQUAB

Squabs, or domestic pigeons, are mild-tasting and tender enough to be split and broiled or roasted. The lime sauce goes perfectly with the mild flavor of the squab. (See photograph on the front cover.)

INGREDIENTS:

½ cup olive oil
½ cup catsup
2 tablespoons granulated sugar
Grated rind of 2 limes
¼ cup lime juice
4 cloves garlic, minced
2 teaspoons Italian herbs
2 tablespoons parsley, chopped
¼ cup wine vinegar
2 tablespoons chopped onion
2 teaspoons dried tarragon or mustard
4 (¾- to 1-pound) squabs, split and flattened
    or (1½-pound) broilers, quartered

PREPARATION:

To prepare the sauce, combine the marinade ingredients in a shallow bowl large enough to hold the fowl. Pour the marinade over the pieces and cover the bowl with a lid or plastic wrap. Refrigerate it for at least 4 hours.

Place the broiler pan on the middle rack and preheat the broiler.

Place the squabs, skin side down, on the broiling pan. Broil them until they are brown, about 7 minutes. Turn them over. Baste with marinade and broil for another 5 minutes. The birds should be crisp and brown.

Place the squabs on warm serving plates. Garnish with slices of lime and serve at once.

4 Servings.

ROAST DUCKLING WITH PINEAPPLE SAUCE

This Pineapple Sauce enhances the flavor of the duck greatly and looks very attractive as well.

INGREDIENTS:

1 (3-pound) duckling
Salt and pepper to taste
1 large onion, chopped
2 tablespoons chopped ginger root
1 tablespoon brown sugar
4 tablespoons soy sauce
4 tablespoons soy oil
1 cup chicken stock
2 tablespoons sherry
4 ounces pineapple juice
2 tablespoons corn flour
2 tablespoons prune jam
4 slices fresh pineapple

PREPARATION:

Wipe the duck well, and rub the inside and outside with salt, pepper, onion and chopped ginger. Mix brown sugar and soy sauce, and paint 3 coats of this mixture on the skin of the duckling. (Collect the excess that drips off the sides to use for the second and third coats.) Let it dry for 30 minutes.

Preheat the oven to 400 degrees.

In a large roasting pan, brown the duckling for 15 minutes. Add the oil and chicken stock to the pan; moisten the duckling with the drippings and roast for 45 minutes, or until the bird is done. (It is tender and the juices run clear when the skin is pierced.) Allow it to cool.

To make the Pineapple Sauce: In a skillet over medium heat, bring the sherry, pineapple juice, corn flour, prune jam and the gravy from the duckling to a boil, stirring constantly. Add the pineapple and cook over low heat for 5 minutes. Remove the pineapple pieces from the sauce and save them for garnish.

Carve the duckling into halves or quarters with poultry shears. Place the pieces on a warmed serving dish. Pour the sauce over the carved duck, and garnish with pineapple slices.

4 Servings.

70

CANARD FLAMBÉ AUX ABRICOTS

(FLAMING DUCKLING WITH APRICOTS)

A flamboyant presentation of a delicious favorite.
(See photograph on page 59.)

INGREDIENTS:

1 (3-pound) duckling, cut into serving pieces
2 tablespoons lemon juice
1 small onion, chopped
1 carrot, finely chopped
1 bay leaf
2 tablespoons all-purpose flour
2 tablespoons lemon juice
½ cup orange juice
½ cup demi-glace*
2 cloves
Salt and pepper to taste
12 apricot halves
4 tablespoons butter
2 tablespoons brown sugar
Orange peel from ½ orange, julienne
3 ounces brandy

PREPARATION:

Preheat the oven to 450 degrees.

In a large skillet over medium heat, place the pieces of duckling skin side down. Sauté until the skin turns golden brown. Turn the pieces and brown them on the other side, for 1 or 2 minutes. Transfer the duck to a baking dish.

Place the dish in the oven and bake for 10 minutes. (This renders the fat from the duck.) Remove the dish and spoon off the fat. Turn the pieces and return the duck to the oven for another 10 minutes.

Remove the pieces from the baking dish and pour off all but 1 tablespoon of fat. Add the onion, carrot and bay leaf to the baking dish and scrape up any bits of meat that have baked onto the bottom. Cook the vegetables for a few minutes.

Return the duck pieces to the baking dish and sprinkle them with a tablespoon of the flour. Turn the pieces over and sprinkle the second side with flour.

Reduce the heat to 350 degrees. Add the juice of the lemon and oranges, the demi-glace, cloves, and salt and pepper. Cover and bake for about 45 minutes. Transfer the duckling pieces to a warm serving platter.

In a skillet, sauté the apricots in butter. Add sugar, orange peel, and the brandy. Light the brandy with a match and pour the flaming sauce over the duck while you shake the pan to spread it out. Keep shaking the pan until the flames are extinguished, and serve immediately.

4 Servings.

---

* *Brown sauce, usually flavored with Madeira or Sherry wine.*

Opposite page: Veal Chops Oscar, recipe on page 73.

Meat

72

Veal Chops Oscar
Veal Scallops California
Veal Scaloppine al Limone
Veal Cordon Bleu
Veal Piccata Lombarda
Osso Buco alla Milanese
Veal Cutlets Parmigiana
Rack of Lamb Boulanger
Lamb Chops "Aussie"
Pork and Apple Pie
Boeuf Bourguignonne
Beef Carbonade Valoise
Beef Stroganoff
Beef Tournedos Rossini
Steak Diane
Calves Liver Lyonnaise

Veal Scallops California, recipe on page 74.

Veal Chops Oscar

A presentation to please the eye as well as the palate. The veal chops are topped with lobster and asparagus spears and a Béarnaise sauce covers all.

INGREDIENTS:

4 veal chops, 8-ounces each
½ cup all-purpose flour
4 tablespoons butter
2 (6-ounce) lobster tails, cooked and cut in half lengthwise
12 asparagus spears, cooked
½ cup Béarnaise Sauce
Salt to taste

PREPARATION:

Preheat the oven to 350 degrees.

Dip the veal in flour, brushing off any excess. Heat the butter in a large heavy skillet and brown the meat quickly on both sides; reduce the heat and continue cooking, for about 5 minutes on each side.

Place the browned chops in a baking dish; remove the lobster meat from the shells and top each piece of meat with half a lobster tail and 3 asparagus spears. Cover with Béarnaise Sauce, and warm for 3 minutes in the preheated oven.

CHEF'S TIP:

Do not overcook veal. It is an exceptionally delicate and tender meat and should be brown on the outside and pink and juicy inside when it is served.

4 Servings.

Béarnaise Sauce:

INGREDIENTS:

4 tablespoons tarragon vinegar
2 tablespoons chopped shallots
4 peppercorns, ground
3 egg yolks
½ cup butter
1 teaspoon tarragon leaves, minced
1 teaspoon chervil, minced

PREPARATION:

In a small saucepan, combine vinegar, shallots and peppercorn. Bring to a boil, cook until 1 tablespoon of liquid remains; pour the liquid through a sieve and allow it to cool.

In a double boiler, beat the egg yolks and add the shallot mixture. Heat the butter to sizzling hot and pour it slowly into the egg yolk mixture, stirring constantly until the sauce turns smooth and thick. Add the tarragon and chervil.

CHEF'S TIP:

Béarnaise Sauce may be prepared ahead of time and stored for a few hours in a tightly closed jar that has been rinsed with hot water.

Makes 1 cup.

74

Veal Scallops California

From sunny California comes this casual but elegant recipe. See photograph on page 72.

INGREDIENTS:

8 veal scallops, 3-ounces each, from the top round
⅓ cup all-purpose flour
Salt and pepper to taste
2 tablespoons butter or margarine
1 garlic clove, finely chopped
2 ounces dry Marsala wine
8 slices fresh ripe tomato
2 ripe avocados
4 thin slices Fontina cheese
4 fresh basil sprigs

PREPARATION:

Lightly flour the veal and season. In a large skillet, melt the butter and sauté the veal, 3 minutes on each side. Set aside.

In the same pan, sauté the garlic, add Marsala wine and cook until it is reduced by half; set aside. Top scallops with tomato slices, 1 per piece. On top, place 3 or 4 slices of avocado and top it with 1 slice of Fontina cheese.

Under the broiler, let the cheese melt. Pour the sauce on to the bottom of the serving platter, place veal on the sauce.

Garnish with the basil sprigs and serve.

4 Servings.

Veal Scaloppine al Limone

Scaloppine of veal is especially prized for its tenderness and light flavor.

INGREDIENTS:

5 tablespoons butter or margarine
2 bay leaves
2 pounds veal tenderloin, trimmed and cut into 24 small thin pieces
2 tablespoons all-purpose flour
Juice of 2 lemons
⅓ cup beef broth
Pinch of Italian herbs
Salt and pepper to taste
4 tablespoons Italian parsley, finely chopped

PREPARATION:

In a large skillet, melt the butter with bay leaves. Sprinkle the veal scallops thoroughly with flour and fry them over high heat for 2 minutes on each side.

Add lemon juice and beef broth to the pan. Stir, and season with Italian herbs, salt and pepper. Just before serving, sprinkle with very moist parsley.

6 Servings.

Veal Cordon Bleu

Prosciutto is an extravagance, but no other ham has its sweet suppleness.

INGREDIENTS:

1½ pounds veal loin, trimmed and cut into
    8 scallops
Salt and pepper to taste
4 slices Swiss cheese, cut and trimmed same
    size as scallops
4 slices prosciutto ham
4 tablespoons all-purpose flour
2 eggs, beaten
1 cup bread crumbs
⅓ cup butter

PREPARATION:

Pound veal scallops ¼-inch thick, working in salt and pepper. Place a slice of cheese and prosciutto atop each scallop. Then top each with another scallop to make a sandwich. Brush the edges of the veal with beaten egg and press them firmly together; trim the edges if necessary.

Sprinkle each with flour, then dip them first in the beaten eggs and then in bread crumbs.

In a large skillet, sauté the veal packets in butter until they are golden brown on both sides.

4 Servings.

Veal Piccata Lombarda

75

Serve these veal scallops with rice, noodles, gnocchi, sautéed potatoes or just a green vegetable or salad.

INGREDIENTS:

¼ cup butter or margarine
2 bay leaves
1½ pounds veal tenderloin scallops, cut into
    16 pieces
1 tablespoon all-purpose flour
½ cup dry white wine
2 ounces pancetta or bacon, cooked and
    chopped
2 cloves garlic, minced
½ teaspoon lemon rind, grated
2 tablespoons parsley, chopped
Salt and pepper to taste

PREPARATION:

In a large skillet, melt the butter; add bay leaves. Drain the veal on paper towels and dredge the pieces in flour. Sauté the veal for 2 minutes on each side. Add the wine; cook for 2 minutes or until the wine evaporates. Add bacon, garlic, lemon rind, parsley and seasonings; stir for 1 more minute. Remove bay leaves and serve.

Serve with Risotto alla Milanese (see page 30).

CHEF'S TIP:

Some people object to flouring veal scallops before cooking. It is optional but it does help the veal to brown better.

4 Servings.

76

OSSO BUCO ALLA MILANESE

(BRAISED SHANK OF VEAL — MILAN STYLE)

One of the really wonderful dishes Milan has given to the world.

INGREDIENTS:

4 pieces veal shank (sawed through including bone with marrow, 10 to 12 ounces each piece)
2 tablespoons all-purpose flour
2 tablespoons cooking oil
4 tablespoons butter
1 each rib of celery, carrot, onion (chopped together)
5 ounces white wine
2 tablespoons tomato purée
1 bay leaf
1 quart beef stock
2 cloves garlic, minced
Lemon zest
Pinch saffron
Pinch rosemary
Salt and pepper to taste
1 tablespoon parsley, chopped

PREPARATION:

Dust the veal pieces with flour and heat the oil and butter in a heavy pan over moderate heat. Brown the veal for 3 minutes on each side, turning the pieces to brown, but keeping them upright to prevent the marrow from falling out.

Reduce the heat and stir in the celery, carrots and onion. Sauté for 10 minutes, stirring occasionally. Moisten with wine. Add tomato purée, bay leaf and beef stock. Cover and simmer for 1½ hours.

Before serving, stir in the garlic, lemon zest, saffron and rosemary. Add salt and pepper to taste. Stir and let it cook for 5 more minutes.

Serve with Risotto alla Milanese (see page 30) or Potato Gnocchi (see page 34).

4 Servings.

VEAL CUTLETS PARMIGIANA

This could well be the main course of a formal Neapolitan party menu.

INGREDIENTS:

2 large eggs, beaten
2 tablespoons milk
Salt and freshly ground black pepper to taste
1 cup bread crumbs
¼ cup grated Parmesan cheese
4 (7-ounce) veal cutlets
6 tablespoons butter or margarine
1 cup Fresh Tomato Sauce
4 slices cooked ham
4 small fresh mozzarella cheese cubes

PREPARATION:

Preheat the oven to 400 degrees.

In a shallow bowl, beat the eggs and milk together. Season with salt and pepper and set aside. In another shallow pan, place the bread crumbs, salt, pepper and grated Parmesan cheese. Set aside.

Place the veal cutlets between layers of waxed paper and pound them until they are very thin. Dip each cutlet into beaten eggs, then coat each with the bread crumb mixture. Press the crumbs into the meat to assure a good coating.

In a large skillet, heat butter or margarine over moderate heat and brown the cutlets on both sides.

Transfer the browned meat to a baking dish, top with Tomato Sauce, the slices of ham and finally the mozzarella. Bake in the oven just until the mozzarella melts.

Serve bubbling hot.

4 Servings.

FRESH TOMATO SAUCE:

INGREDIENTS:

5 ripe plum tomatoes
1 rib celery, chopped
1 small onion, chopped
1 small carrot, chopped
¼ cup water
1 bay leaf
½ teaspoon salt
2 cloves garlic
Bouquet garni (fresh parsley and basil)

PREPARATION:

In a large pan, simmer all the sauce ingredients for 1 hour; remove the bay leaf and strain through a sieve, or blend in a food processor.

Makes about 2 cups.

78

Rack of Lamb Boulanger, recipe on opposite page.

RACK OF LAMB BOULANGER

Welcome spring with this fabulous dish on your dinner menu.

INGREDIENTS:

2 small onions, sliced
2 russet potatoes, peeled and sliced
5 tablespoons olive oil
2 racks of lamb (about 6 to 8 chops each)*
1 pound ripe tomatoes, chopped
4 garlic cloves, crushed
½ cup dry white wine
2 tablespoons chopped Italian parsley
Pinch each of oregano, thyme, marjoram,
   rosemary
Salt to taste

PREPARATION:

Preheat the oven to 500 degrees.

In a shallow baking pan, toss onions and potatoes with 4 tablespoons of olive oil. Bake for 10 minutes in the oven.

Brush the racks of lamb with 1 tablespoon of oil and place them on top of the potatoes and onions.

In a bowl, mix together tomatoes, garlic, wine, parsley, herbs and salt; stir well. Pour the mixture over the lamb and cook for 10 minutes. Decrease the temperature to 400 degrees and bake for another 15 minutes for rare lamb.

Transfer to a warm platter. Carve into chops and serve.

4 Servings.

---

* **Note:** *Have the butcher french the ribs for you.*

LAMB CHOPS "AUSSIE"

79

The finest lamb is imported from New Zealand or Australia. It is called "spring lamb" although it is available year-round.

INGREDIENTS:

4 tablespoons bread crumbs, plain
1 tablespoon chopped parsley
2 tablespoons Parmesan cheese, grated
2 tablespoons olive oil
1 tablespoon Dijon mustard
Salt and pepper
6 tablespoons butter or margarine
8 (4-ounces each) double lamb chops
1 ounce dry sherry

PREPARATION:

Preheat the oven to 400 degrees.

In a bowl, combine the bread crumbs, parsley, cheese, oil, mustard, and seasonings; mix well to prepare a *"panure"* or coating. Set aside.

In a heavy skillet, heat the butter and brown the chops for about 4 minutes on each side. They should be crusty on the outside and pink on the inside. Sprinkle with sherry.

Place ⅛ of the cheese mixture on top of each lamb chop. Spread the mixture over the surface. Place the chops in a baking dish and bake for 4 minutes.

4 Servings.

80 PORK AND APPLE PIE

A different way to make the traditional combination of pork and apple.

INGREDIENTS:

¾ cup butter or margarine
1 large onion, chopped
1½ pounds boneless pork, diced
2 cooking apples, peeled and diced
1 teaspoon thyme
1 tablespoon A-1 sauce
2 tablespoons parsley, chopped
1 tablespoon cornstarch
½ cup warm water
2 ounces dry sherry
1 pie shell, 9-inch diameter
2 large potatoes, cooked
½ cup milk
Salt and pepper to taste
Pinch of nutmeg

PREPARATION:

In a large skillet, with ¼ cup of the butter and the chopped onion, brown the pork. Reduce the heat and simmer for 30 minutes. Add apples, thyme, A-1 sauce and parsley; continue cooking for 15 minutes.

Dilute cornstarch with warm water and pour onto pork. Stir well, add sherry and remove from the heat. Pour into the pie shell.

In a separate bowl, mash the potatoes with ¼ cup of the butter and milk; add salt and pepper to taste and a pinch of nutmeg. Spread over the pork mixture to cover. Dot the potatoes with the remaining butter. Bake in the

Pork and Apple Pie.

oven at 350 degrees for 25 minutes or until golden brown.

CHEF'S TIP:

For an attractive way to spread the mashed potatoes, spoon it into a pastry tube with a wide tip, and pipe potatoes onto the pork mixture.

6 Servings.

BOEUF BOURGUIGNONNE

One of the most popular of all braised beef dishes, this French beef stew is especially suitable for winter buffet tables.

INGREDIENTS:

6 strips bacon, chopped
2 tablespoons olive oil
1 medium-sized carrot, chopped
1 medium-sized onion, chopped
1 rib celery, chopped
2 tablespoons butter or margarine
1½ pounds lean beef, cubed
3 tablespoons all-purpose flour
2 ounces brandy
1 cup red or burgundy wine
2 cups beef stock
2 cloves garlic
Bouquet garni (parsley, celery, thyme, bay leaf)
Salt and pepper
12 small white onions, peeled
12 firm white mushroom caps
½ cup water
Juice of 1 lemon
1 teaspoon sugar
1 tablespoon butter or margarine
Burgundy wine

PREPARATION:

In a large skillet, sauté bacon, oil and chopped vegetables; add butter. Dredge the beef with flour; add it to the skillet, and mix it with the browned vegetables. Stir and cook for 5 minutes. Add brandy, wine, beef stock, garlic, the bouquet garni and salt and pepper to taste. Simmer gently for 1½ hours. If the sauce is too

Boeuf Bourguignonne.

thin, you can thicken it by adding 2 tablespoons of flour blended with 1 tablespoon of butter.

Serve with pearl onions and mushrooms that have been cooked for about 5 minutes in water, lemon juice, and sugar. Drain and sauté the onions and mushrooms in butter and a little burgundy wine.

4 Servings.

82

BEEF CARBONADE VALOISE

Delicious and quite easy to prepare.

INGREDIENTS:

**2 tablespoons butter or margarine
3 strips bacon, chopped
4 (8-ounce) sirloin or spencer steaks
1 large onion, sliced
1 lemon rind
3 cloves garlic, minced
1 tablespoon all-purpose flour
2 tablespoons cider vinegar
3 tablespoons brown sugar
1 can dark beer
1 cup beef stock
1 clove
1 tablespoon parsley, chopped
Pinch of thyme
Freshly ground pepper
Salt to taste**

PREPARATION:

In a large skillet, combine butter and bacon; sauté steaks for 2 minutes on each side; add onion, lemon rind and garlic. Stir twice; remove from heat and pour off any remaining fat.

Adjust the heat to medium. Sprinkle with flour and add all the remaining ingredients. Cover and simmer for 45 minutes in the sauce.

Serve with Potato Gnocchi (see page 34).

4 Servings.

BEEF STROGANOFF

This Russian-style recipe is quick to prepare and widely enjoyed as a party dish. Serve it with sautéed mushrooms and noodles.

INGREDIENTS:

**1½ pounds lean beef fillet
Salt and freshly ground black pepper to taste
4 tablespoons butter
1 tablespoon all-purpose flour
1 cup beef broth
1 teaspoon prepared mustard
1 onion, sliced
¼ cup dairy sour cream, at room temperature
Chopped parsley for garnish**

PREPARATION:

Cut the fillets into narrow strips about 2-inches long and 1-inch thick. Season the strips with salt and pepper and refrigerate them for 2 hours.

In a saucepan, melt 2 tablespoons of the butter; add the flour and stir with a wooden spoon until blended. Meanwhile, bring the broth to a boil and add all at once to the butter/flour mixture, stirring vigorously until the sauce is thickened and smooth. Stir in the mustard.

In a separate pan, heat the remaining butter, add the meat and sliced onion and brown quickly on both sides.

To serve, remove the meat to a hot platter, discarding the onion and meat juices. Add the sour cream to the mustard sauce and simmer gently for 3 minutes. Pour sauce over meat and garnish with parsley.

4 Servings.

Beef Tournedos Rossini.

BEEF TOURNEDOS ROSSINI 83

Tournedos are small steaks made from filet mignon, the tenderest and most luxurious part of the beef.

INGREDIENTS:

4 (8-ounce) beef tenderloin medallions
6 tablespoons butter
**4 slices pâté de foie gras* (2½-inches in
    diameter, ½-inch thick)**
2 tablespoons all-purpose flour
**4 slices white or black truffle, (1-inch
    diameter)**
6 ounces Madeira wine
Salt and pepper to taste

PREPARATION:

In a large skillet, heat 4 tablespoons of the butter, sauté the meat for 5 minutes on each side. Transfer to an oven-proof serving dish and place it in a warm oven.

Add the remaining butter to the skillet. Coat the *fois de gras* medallions with flour and sauté on both sides very quickly. Place one on top of each tournedo and garnish each of them with a slice of truffle.

Pour the wine into the skillet, and bring it to a boil; stir and cook until the liquid thickens. Pour this sauce over the tournedos and serve.

---

*Tins of Pâté de Foie Gras (French goose liver paté with truffles) are available in most gourmet grocery stores.

4 Servings.

84   Steak Diane

Quick and easy does it. With your choice of vegetables and Chilled Strawberry Soufflé (see page 133), your meal is ready in minutes.

INGREDIENTS:

4 tender (6- to 8-ounce) lean sirloin steaks
6 tablespoons butter
¼ cup chopped shallots
1 tablespoon Worcestershire sauce
5 ounces brandy, warm
Salt and freshly ground pepper
Dijon mustard (optional)

PREPARATION:

Pound the tender steaks to ⅓-inch thickness.

In a large skillet, melt the butter and, using high heat, sauté the steaks for 3 minutes on each side. Add shallots and stir for 1 minute. Add Worcestershire sauce and then flame with warm brandy. Add salt and pepper and 1 teaspoon of Dijon mustard, if desired.

Serve the steaks at once on a warmed platter. Pour the sauce remaining in the pan over the steaks.

4 Servings.

Calves Liver Lyonnaise

Prepared with onions, this is a delicacy originating in Lyons, France, a capital of the pleasures of the table.

INGREDIENTS:

2 tablespoons cooking oil
4 tablespoons butter
2 onions, julienne
1 bay leaf
⅓ cup red wine
All-purpose flour
2 pounds calves liver, thinly sliced
1 tablespoon cider vinegar
Salt
Freshly ground pepper
Chopped parsley

PREPARATION:

In a large skillet using the oil and 2 tablespoons of the butter, sauté the onions until they are transparent, and add the bay leaf and wine. Reduce the heat and cook slowly until the wine is evaporated. Spoon the onions into a dish and set aside.

Dredge the liver slices in flour. In the skillet, melt the remaining butter, brown the liver quickly on both sides. Sprinkle with vinegar and seasonings; cover the liver with the sautéed onion. Cook for 2 more minutes and serve on a warm platter.

CHEF'S TIP:

Liver should be served slightly pink. If it is overcooked, it becomes grainy.

6 Servings.

Opposite page: Salade Niçoise, recipe on page 92.

SALADS

86

Curried Chicken Salad
Luisa Lago Chicken Salad
Fresh Tuna Steak Caprese
Salmón en Escabeche
Russian Salmon Salad
Shrimp Salad Riviera
Lobster Salad
Avocado with Crabmeat
King Crabmeat Salad Plate
Salade Niçoise
Caesar Salad
Coleslaw
Red Cabbage Salad
Dutch Cucumber Salad
Waldorf Salad
Salad Mimosa

Luisa Lago Chicken Salad, recipe on opposite page.

CURRIED CHICKEN SALAD

Chicken salad is the most popular of all the main dish salads. This one would be ideal especially for those who enjoy the curry flavor and its customary partners—raisins, coconut, apples, bananas, grapes and cashews.

INGREDIENTS:

1 cup diced cold chicken
1 cup rice pilaf, cold
¼ cup golden raisins
2 tablespoons shredded coconut
2 tablespoons Indian cashews, chopped
2 apples, peeled and cubed
1 tablespoon lemon juice
1 tablespoon curry powder
4 tablespoons dairy sour cream
Salt and pepper to taste
Salad greens
Bananas and red grapes for garnish

PREPARATION:

Combine the first 10 ingredients. Toss and divide into 4 individual servings.

Serve on a bed of greens, garnished with peeled, sliced banana and red grapes.

4 Servings.

LUISA LAGO CHICKEN SALAD

This salade composée won high praises for its flavor, color and texture.

INGREDIENTS:

1 whole chicken breast, roasted, skinned, boned and sliced julienne
1 celery heart, cut into small cubes
1 Granny Smith apple, cut into small cubes
2 medium-sized carrots, julienne
1 (4-ounce) head red raddichio, julienne
½ cup chopped walnuts
1 fresh ginger root, about 3 ounces, peeled and chopped, or ½ teaspoon powdered ginger
Mustard Vinaigrette Dressing
1 large orange, peeled and sliced for garnish

PREPARATION:

In a salad bowl, combine the chicken, celery, apple, carrots, raddichio, walnuts and ginger. Add the vinaigrette and toss gently until the ingredients are well coated. Cover the bowl and chill for at least an hour.

For the Mustard Vinaigrette Dressing: In a small bowl, beat together 1 tablespoon Dijon mustard, 1 tablespoon granulated sugar, 1 tablespoon mayonnaise, 1 tablespoon balsamic vinegar, 2 tablespoons olive oil, dash of Tabasco sauce, and salt to taste, until the ingredients are well blended; or shake vigorously in a jar with a tight lid.

Serve on individual salad plates or in bowls. Garnish with orange slices.

4 Servings.

FRESH TUNA STEAK CAPRESE

88

These baked tuna steaks, marinated and topped with the lively sauce, make a delightful warm weather entrée.

INGREDIENTS:

6 (7-ounce) tuna steaks
Juice of 2 lemons
Salt and pepper to taste
1 teaspoon Italian herbs
3 tablespoons olive oil
2 pounds fresh ripe tomatoes, peeled and
    chopped
3 cloves chopped garlic
1 tablespoon chopped capers
1 medium-sized red onion, chopped
2 cups dry white wine
3 tablespoons chopped parsley

PREPARATION:

Marinate the tuna steak with lemon juice, salt, pepper and half of the Italian herbs for at least 2 hours; then bake for 20 minutes at 350 degrees. Allow to cool.

In a salad bowl, mix the oil with the tomatoes, garlic, capers, onion, and the remaining Italian herbs. Finally, add the dry white wine and top the tuna steak with this cold sauce before serving. Garnish with the parsley. Serve cold.

6 Servings.

SALMÓN EN ESCABECHE

Escabeche is the Spanish word for "pickled." Serve this cold marinated salmon as the main course on a summer day.

INGREDIENTS:

⅓ cup olive oil
1½ pounds fresh salmon fillet, cut into
    3- by 1-inch pieces
⅓ cup all-purpose flour
3 tablespoons olive oil
1 medium-sized onion, julienne
6 cloves garlic, crushed
2 bay leaves
1 ounce fresh rosemary
2 teaspoons black peppercorns
½ cup wine vinegar
⅓ cup dry white wine
Salt to taste
Lime wedges, cucumber slices and dill sprigs
    for garnish

PREPARATION:

Preheat the oil in a medium skillet; dust the salmon with flour, and sauté it in the oil, turning to brown both sides.

Transfer the fish to a salad bowl. Pour off any remaining oil and wipe the skillet. Using the 3 tablespoons oil, sauté the onion until it is transparent. Add garlic, bay leaves, rosemary and peppercorns; stir and cook until the garlic turns brown. Pour in vinegar and wine; bring the mixture to a boil and pour over the top of the salmon. Let the fish marinate in the refrigerator for at least 2 hours before serving.

To serve, drain excess marinade. Place the fish on a serving platter, lined with lettuce, and garnish with slices of lime and cucumber and sprigs of dill.

6 Servings

RUSSIAN SALMON SALAD

This luncheon salad brings together a happy marriage of flavors and colors.

INGREDIENTS:

½ cup poached salmon flakes
1 cup cooked potatoes, diced
¼ cup chopped gherkins
¼ cup cooked carrots, diced
1 sprig fresh dill, or 1 teaspoon dried dill
1½ cups mayonnaise
4 hard-cooked eggs, cut in wedges
4 slices lemon
1 roasted red pepper, julienne
1 tablespoon tomato purée

PREPARATION:

Combine salmon with potatoes, gherkins, carrots, dill and 1 cup of the mayonnaise. Mix well.

To serve, spoon the salad onto a bed of greens on a serving platter and garnish with egg wedges, lemon slices and red pepper strips.

Mix together the remaining mayonnaise with tomato purée, using this sauce for more decoration.

4 Servings.

SHRIMP SALAD RIVIERA

Nothing could be finer for a luncheon on the Riviera, or in your own home.

INGREDIENTS:

2 egg yolks
2 tablespoons lemon juice
1 teaspoon granulated sugar
Salt and pepper
2 tablespoons olive oil
12 medium-sized shrimp cooked, peeled and deveined
2 heads red radicchio, cut in small wedges
1 fennel (anise), bulb section, cut in wedges
1 red bell pepper, cleaned and cut in thin strips
1 cup arugola
½ cup mushrooms, sliced
12 red radishes with tender leaves, pared as roses for garnish

PREPARATION:

For the dressing: Beat the egg yolks with lemon juice, sugar, salt and pepper and oil until smooth.

Toss the remaining ingredients with the exception of the radishes. Serve on individual salad plates, garnished with radish roses.

CHEF'S TIP:

To make a radish rose, use a sharp paring knife to cut very thin petals of red radish skin down, but not through, the radish top. Drop them in a bowl of water with ice in it and they will open and become very crisp.

4 Servings.

90

LOBSTER SALAD

Fresh cooked lobster meat is found in most seafood markets. Use it the same day for this savory salad.

INGREDIENTS:

**12 ounces cooked lobster meat, cut in
 ¾-inch chunks
1 cup diced boiled potatoes
1 cup diced giardiniera (marinated
 vegetables)
1 tablespoon chopped capers, washed and
 drained
4 tablespoons olive oil
2 tablespoons mayonnaise
2 tablespoons chopped parsley
2 tablespoons lemon juice
Salt and freshly ground pepper
Red beets and yellow pepper, julienne,
 for garnish**

PREPARATION:

Combine lobster, potatoes, *giardiniera* and capers.

For the dressing: Mix the oil, mayonnaise, parsley, lemon juice, salt and pepper.

Toss with the lobster salad mixture and serve on salad plates lined with greens.

Garnish with julienned red beets and yellow pepper.

4 Servings.

AVOCADO WITH CRABMEAT

This salad makes a complete luncheon dish or may be served in small portions, as a first course for dinner.

INGREDIENTS:

**½ pound cooked Alaska King crabmeat flakes
2 tablespoons lemon juice
1 tablespoon chili sauce
1 tablespoon capers, washed and drained
Dash of Tabasco sauce
Salt to taste
2 medium-sized ripe avocados
4 tablespoons mayonnaise
1 red pepper, roasted and finely sliced**

PREPARATION:

Combine the crabmeat, lemon juice, chili sauce, capers, Tabasco sauce and salt in a bowl. Mix well and marinate the mixture for 1 hour.

Cut the avocados in half vertically and remove the seed. Scoop out the pulp and cut it into small cubes. Reserve the avocado shells for serving. Add the avocado cubes to the marinated mixture and mix them in gently and slowly.

To serve, fill avocado shells with salad; spread 1 tablespoon of mayonnaise over the salad mixture in each shell. Garnish with red pepper slices and place each shell on a bed of greens.

CHEF'S TIP:

Maryland and Florida lump crabmeat are a superb substitute for the Alaska King crabmeat.

4 Servings.

King Crabmeat Salad Plate.

KING CRABMEAT SALAD PLATE

An exquisite array of tempting foods.

INGREDIENTS:

**2 hard-cooked eggs, peeled and cut in halves,
  yolk removed**
1 teaspoon capers, washed and drained
2 tablespoons dairy sour cream
4 teaspoons red salmon caviar
**10 ounces cooked Alaska King crabmeat
  flakes**
4 tablespoons mayonnaise
4 or 5 large Boston lettuce leaves
2 medium-sized tomatoes, cut in wedges
**½ pound asparagus spears, steamed and
  chilled**

PREPARATION:

Combine the egg yolks, capers and sour
cream; mash the mixture with a fork until it is
smooth, and fill the egg white halves; top them
with red caviar.

Mix the crabmeat and mayonnaise.

To serve, place the crabmeat salad in
the center of a round serving dish. Surround
with lettuce leaves, tomato wedges, asparagus
spears and stuffed eggs.

4 Servings.

92

SALADE NIÇOISE

This is a salad that originated in the vicinity of Nice. It makes marvelous use of the regional specialties — tuna from the Mediterranean, and olives and fresh vegetables from the surrounding countryside.

INGREDIENTS:

1 head romaine lettuce, broken into 1-inch
    pieces
¼ cup olive oil
2 tablespoons lemon juice
Salt and pepper to taste
½ teaspoon herbs (oregano, thyme)
1 tablespoon chopped parsley
2 small tomatoes, cut in half and sliced
6 anchovy fillets, cut in small pieces
½ pound cooked string beans
½ cup small pitted black olives
1 small onion, cut in half and sliced
1 (6-ounce) can light tuna in olive oil,
    drained, cut in small chunks
2 hard-cooked eggs, quartered
¼ cup sliced cucumbers

PREPARATION:

Wash and dry the romaine lettuce. Wrap it in a dish towel or paper towels, and refrigerate it.

For the dressing: In a salad bowl combine oil, lemon juice, salt, pepper, herbs and parsley; mix well.

Toss the romaine lettuce, tomatoes, anchovies, beans, olives and onion; mix well.

Divide into 4 portions, top with tuna and garnish with egg quarters and cucumber slices.

4 Servings.

CAESAR SALAD

This classic salad is a West Coast favorite.

INGREDIENTS:

2 heads romaine lettuce
1 cup diced, firm white bread
½ cup olive oil
2 cloves garlic, peeled and crushed
1 clove garlic, peeled
2 tablespoons lemon juice
½ teaspoon dry mustard
3 egg yolks
Dash of Worcestershire sauce
4 anchovy fillets, cut in small pieces
¼ cup grated Parmesan cheese

PREPARATION:

Wash and dry the romaine lettuce. Wrap it in a dish towel or paper towels, and refrigerate it.

To make croutons: Sauté the diced bread in ¼ cup of the olive oil with the crushed garlic cloves until the croutons are golden brown and crisp. Remove the garlic and drain the croutons on absorbent paper.

Rub a chilled salad bowl with the garlic.

For the dressing: Combine ¼ cup of the oil, lemon, mustard, egg and Worcestershire sauce; mix well for one minute. Pour into the salad bowl. Break the greens into bite-sized pieces, and add them to the bowl. Toss well so that each lettuce leaf is coated. Add the anchovies and croutons to the bowl. Toss again and sprinkle with the grated cheese.

4 Servings.

Caesar Salad, recipe on opposite page.

94

COLESLAW

Ever since people learned to shred cabbage, cole-slaw recipes have been rapidly multiplying. Here is Princess Cruises' chefs' choice with variations.

INGREDIENTS:

⅓ cup dairy sour cream
¼ cup mayonnaise
3 tablespoons vinegar
1 tablespoon granulated sugar
½ teaspoon dry mustard
¼ teaspoon freshly ground pepper
Salt
½ medium-sized head white cabbage,
    shredded
3 tablespoons chopped onion
1 carrot, grated

PREPARATION:

Mix sour cream, mayonnaise, vinegar, sugar and seasoning. Toss with cabbage, onion and grated carrot.

For variety, add some dill if desired, or omit the onion and substitute a Granny Smith apple, peeled and chopped, or you can add 2 ounces of crumbled blue cheese.

6 Servings.

RED CABBAGE SALAD

A delicious balance of sweet and sour flavors enhance this crunchy salad.

INGREDIENTS:

½ head red cabbage, shredded
1 celery root
⅓ cup cider vinegar
2 tablespoons granulated sugar
3 tablespoons olive oil
2 teaspoons horseradish cream
1 medium-sized onion, chopped
1 tablespoon caraway seed
3 tablespoons chopped nuts
Salt and pepper to taste

PREPARATION:

Parboil shredded cabbage in salted water for 3 minutes and drain it well.

In a small saucepan, boil the celery root until it is tender; allow it to cool and cut it into small cubes.

In a salad bowl, combine vinegar, sugar, oil and horseradish cream. Mix well. Add onion, celery root and cabbage and toss until the dressing covers all the vegetables.

Sprinkle with caraway seeds and nuts.

4 Servings.

Waldorf Salad.

DUTCH CUCUMBER SALAD

Cucumbers are a particularly good accompaniment to salmon dishes.

INGREDIENTS:

**4 medium-sized cucumbers, peeled and
   thinly sliced
1 tablespoon salt
¾ cup dairy sour cream
2 tablespoons cider vinegar
2 tablespoons granulated sugar
½ teaspoon lemon rind, grated
1 tablespoon chopped onion
⅓ cup chopped chives
1 tablespoon chopped parsley
Freshly ground pepper to taste**

PREPARATION:

Combine the sliced cucumbers with salt; let stand for 2 hours, then drain them thoroughly.

In a bowl, combine sour cream, vinegar, sugar and lemon rind, and mix well. Just before serving, toss in the cucumbers, onion, chives, parsley and freshly ground pepper. Salad should be moist, but with no liquid.

4 Servings.

WALDORF SALAD

This salad, made of apples and walnuts has become as well known as the Waldorf Hotel in New York where, presumably, it got its start.

INGREDIENTS:

**2 tablespoons lemon juice
4 apples, unpeeled and diced
4 ribs tender white celery, diced
½ cup walnuts, chopped
3 tablespoons mayonnaise
3 tablespoons whipped cream
3 tablespoons dairy sour cream
Lettuce leaves
1 dozen walnut halves and red apple wedges,
   for garnish**

PREPARATION:

Sprinkle the lemon juice over the diced apples to prevent them from turning dark in color.

Combine the apples, celery, chopped nuts, mayonnaise, whipped and sour cream.

Divide into 4 individual salad bowls lined with lettuce leaves. Garnish each bowl with 3 walnut halves and a few wedges of red apples.

4 Servings.

96

SALAD MIMOSA

Fruit macedoines, or salads, can be made up of almost any assortment of fruits, but the best results usually come from a sampling of only a few, as in this recipe.

INGREDIENTS:

2 heads Boston lettuce
½ cup white grapes, seedless
1 cup orange segments
½ cup sliced banana
4 egg yolks, hard-cooked and chopped
1 tablespoon chopped parsley

PREPARATION:

Wash and dry the lettuce. Wrap it in paper towels or a dish towel until just before you serve the salad.

To serve, combine lettuce, broken into large pieces, grapes, orange segments, and sliced banana in a salad bowl.

Toss the fruit salad with the dressing and serve it in 4 individual bowls. Garnish with chopped egg yolks and parsley.

FRUIT SALAD DRESSING:

INGREDIENTS:

2 tablespoons mayonnaise
2 tablespoons olive oil
2 tablespoons lemon juice
1 tablespoon granulated sugar
1 tablespoon French mustard
Salt and pepper

PREPARATION:

In a blender, mix the mayonnaise, oil, lemon juice, sugar, mustard, salt and pepper.

CHEF'S TIP:

Raw fruit will taste best if it is removed from the refrigerator about an hour before serving time and allowed to warm to room temperature. Chilling keeps fruits fresh, but it also lessens their flavor.

4 Servings.

Opposite page: Pissaladière, recipe on page 99.

OTHER ENTRÉES
AND DISHES

98

Pissaladière
Valdostana Cheese Fondue
Tomatoes Filled with Fondue
Caprice des Dieux Soufflé
Cheese Pudding
Angel Hair Frittata
Fried Eggplant Pizzaiola
Ratatouille
Chalupas
Tacos con Jamón y Queso
Enchiladas
Moussaka
Savory Cabbage Rolls
Nasi Goreng
Malay Satay
Banane Beignets au Curaçao Liqueur Sauce
Blueberry Crumb Muffins
Cinnamon Scones

Valdostana Cheese Fondue, recipe on page 100.

PISSALADIÈRE

This is a flan mainly found in the Nice region of France. Ours features onions, tomatoes, cheese, olives and herbs. It is equally good as the main dish of a light lunch, or as a first course tempting tidbit.

THE DOUGH:

INGREDIENTS:

1 envelope (¼-ounce) active dry yeast
1 cup warm water (105 to 115 degrees)
½ teaspoon salt
2 cups all-purpose flour
2 tablespoons olive oil

PREPARATION:

Grease a 12-inch round baking pan.

In a small bowl, dissolve the yeast in ¼ cup of the warm water. Measure the flour and salt into a large mixing bowl. Add the dissolved yeast, olive oil and ½ cup of the warm water. Mix well to form a ball of dough, adding more water if necessary.

Place the dough on a lightly-floured surface and knead it for about 5 minutes until it is smooth and elastic. Spread oil in the mixing bowl, and turn the ball of dough in it to grease it. Cover the bowl and let the dough rise in a warm place until it doubles in size, about 2 hours. Punch the dough down, and spread it over the bottom of the baking pan. Cover and set it aside while you prepare the filling.

THE FILLING:

INGREDIENTS:

6 tablespoons olive oil
3 cloves garlic, minced
1 large onion, finely sliced
1½ pounds fresh plum tomatoes, chopped
1 teaspoon dry herbs (thyme, oregano, marjoram)
½ cup grated Parmesan cheese
½ cup pitted black olives, sliced

PREPARATION:

Preheat the oven to 375 degrees.

In a large skillet, heat 3 tablespoons of the oil, and sauté the garlic and onion slices until they are translucent; then add the tomatoes and herbs, and simmer at moderate heat for 20 minutes.

Cool the sauce slightly, and spread it evenly on the dough. Sprinkle on the Parmesan cheese. Decorate with sliced olives, and drizzle the remaining oil over the top.

Bake the *pissaladière* in the preheated oven for 25 to 30 minutes, until the edges are brown. Serve it hot.

4 Servings.

VALDOSTANA CHEESE FONDUE

100

This fondue is named after the Valle d'Aosta, in the Piedmont region of Italy, noted for its good cheeses — especially Fontina.

INGREDIENTS:

5 ounces half-and-half
10 ounces Fontina cheese, cut in small cubes
2 ounces dry white wine
Salt and freshly ground pepper to taste
1 teaspoon white truffles, finely minced
4 egg yolks

PREPARATION:

In the top of a double boiler or a fondue pot, combine the half-and-half and cheese and stir occasionally, until the cheese is melted and creamy. Add the wine, salt and pepper and stir a few more minutes.

Just before serving, stir in the truffles and egg yolks, one at a time.

Serve with slices of bread toast or bread croutons, speared onto long-handled forks.

4 Servings.

TOMATOES FILLED WITH FONDUE

Serve with a crisp green salad for a light lunch or supper.

INGREDIENTS:

8 medium-sized tomatoes, peeled
Salt
2 tablespoons butter
¼ cup Swiss cheese, grated
2 tablespoons dry sherry
1 tablespoon French mustard
Dash of Tabasco sauce
Pinch of nutmeg
Pinch of salt
1 tablespoon chopped parsley
3 tablespoons croutons

PREPARATION:

Preheat the oven to 400 degrees.

Cut off tomato tops, scoop a teaspoon of pulp out of each one, and sprinkle them with salt. Leave them to drain in a small skillet.

In a saucepan over medium heat, stir the butter and cheese until it melts. Then add the sherry, mustard, Tabasco sauce, nutmeg and salt and stir for 2 more minutes; add the parsley. Fill the tomatoes with the cheese mixture. Arrange the filled tomatoes in a baking dish with a small amount of water in the bottom. Bake in the oven for 25 minutes. Garnish with croutons.

CHEF'S TIP:

To peel tomatoes, boil 2 cups of water in a medium-sized saucepan and immerse the tomatoes for about 1 minute.

4 Servings.

CAPRICE DES DIEUX SOUFFLÉ

The cheese soufflé is the epitome of French cuisine. It is not difficult to prepare and needs only a light salad as an accompaniment.

INGREDIENTS:

2 tablespoons butter
2 tablespoons all-purpose flour
½ cup milk at boiling point
Salt and pepper to taste
Pinch of nutmeg
3 egg yolks
4 egg whites
3 ounces Caprice des Dieux or Camembert,
** cut in small cubes**

PREPARATION:

Preheat the oven to 350 degrees.

In a small saucepan, melt butter, blend in the flour with a wooden spoon, and stir over moderate heat for 2 minutes, to make a *roux*.

Remove the pan from the heat, and let it cool a moment. Using a wire whip, add the hot milk all at once, beating vigorously. Add salt and nutmeg, stir for a few minutes. Remove from heat and allow it to cool while you separate the eggs, dropping the whites into a mixing bowl, and dropping the yolks, one by one into the hot sauce, stirring them in.

Beat the egg whites until they are stiff, and fold them into the egg yolk mixture with a spatula.

Pour the mixture into greased individual soufflé dishes, top with cheese and bake at 350 degrees for 10 minutes. Adjust heat to 400 degrees and bake until brown, approximately 10 to 12 minutes.

Serve these soufflés plain or with sherry sauce.

4 Servings.

CHEESE PUDDING

This is a very good, but very rich pudding. A little goes a long way.

INGREDIENTS:

1 cup fresh white bread crumbs
1 quart milk
Dash of salt and pepper
Pinch each of nutmeg and marjoram
1 pound Cheddar cheese, grated
4 strips bacon, crispy and chopped
4 eggs, beaten
3 tablespoons butter
1 tablespoon all-purpose flour

PREPARATION:

Preheat the oven to 350 degrees.

Soften the bread crumbs in milk. Add the salt and spices and let the crumbs soften for half an hour. Add the cheese, bacon and eggs. Pour into a greased, floured casserole.

Bake for 1 hour.

8 Servings.

102 ANGEL HAIR FRITTATA

A glorious Italian omelet with vegetables and pasta.

INGREDIENTS:

4 tablespoons butter or margarine
4 tablespoons olive oil
2 cloves garlic, minced
¼ cup sliced fresh mushrooms
2 small zucchini, thinly sliced
¼ cup chopped ripe tomatoes
Pinch each of thyme and oregano
Salt and pepper
10 ounces angel hair noodles cooked for
  4 minutes and drained
2 eggs
4 tablespoons grated Romano cheese

PREPARATION:

In a small skillet, heat the butter and 2 tablespoons of the oil; sauté the garlic until golden. Add the mushrooms and zucchini stirring occasionally for 5 minutes; stir in tomatoes, herbs, salt and pepper. Cook for 20 more minutes. Allow it to cool slightly.

Toss the cooked pasta with the mushrooms, zucchini and tomato mixture.

Beat the eggs in a bowl and add the Romano cheese. Add the pasta and vegetable mixture.

In a 9-inch skillet, warm the remaining oil until it is very hot. Pour in the pasta and egg mixture and stir for 2 minutes. Reduce the heat to medium and cook for 3 minutes until the eggs have set. The top may still be a bit runny. Use a 10-inch dinner plate to turn the mixture and cook on the other side for 5 more minutes.

Frittata is ready to serve hot or cold, as you prefer.

4 Servings.

FRIED EGGPLANT PIZZAIOLA

Make these little sandwiches from eggplant and mozzarella cheese for a pungent snack.

INGREDIENTS:

1 eggplant, firm and seedless, about
    2½-inches in diameter
Salt
4 ripe plum tomatoes, chopped
1 clove garlic, minced
Salt and pepper
Pinch of oregano
4 mozzarella "Bocconcini" (about 4-ounces
    each)
8 anchovy fillets
2 tablespoons all-purpose flour
1 cup bread crumbs
2 eggs, beaten
1 cup olive oil

PREPARATION:

Slice the eggplant into 16 round thin slices. Sprinkle them with salt and place them on paper towels to rest for 1 hour. Then, squeeze them to remove the dark bitter liquid.

103

In a small bowl, combine the tomatoes, garlic, salt, pepper and oregano.

Cut the mozzarella cheese into 8 slices. Dip each slice in the tomato mixture and make sandwiches by combining 2 slices of eggplant, 1 slice of mozzarella cheese and 1 anchovy fillet. Press them together and dust with flour.

In a small bowl, combine bread crumbs and eggs. Heat the oil in a deep skillet. Dip the sandwiches in the batter and fry the eggplant pizzaiola until they are golden brown and crusty. Serve at once.

4 Servings.

104

Ratatouille.

RATATOUILLE

(PROVENÇALE VEGETABLE CASSEROLE)

From Nice, Ratatouille has become an international favorite to accompany fish or meat.

INGREDIENTS:

5 tablespoons olive oil
2 medium-sized onions, cut in half, then sliced
4 garlic cloves, crushed
3 zucchini, cut in 1-inch cubes
2 green bell peppers, cut in large pieces
1 large, firm, seedless eggplant, peeled and cut in 1-inch cubes
6 ripe tomatoes, chopped
½ teaspoon basil
½ teaspoon marjoram
½ teaspoon oregano
½ teaspoon thyme
Salt to taste
Freshly ground pepper

PREPARATION:

In a large saucepan, heat the oil and sauté the onions and garlic until the onions are translucent. Add the zucchini, peppers and eggplant. Mix well, cover the pan and simmer for 10 minutes, tossing the vegetables a few times so they cook evenly. Add the tomatoes and seasonings and continue to cook over low heat for another 10 minutes. Uncover the pan and allow the liquid to reduce, stirring frequently for approximately 5 minutes. Adjust the seasonings to suit your taste.

Serve hot or cold with crusty bread.

4 Servings.

CHALUPAS

An enjoyable Mexican dish, Chalupas means "little boats." Serve it with fresh fruit to complete a substantial meal.

INGREDIENTS:

4 corn tortillas
2 tablespoons vegetable oil or bacon drippings
1 cup mashed black beans
2 ripe tomatoes in chunks
1 tablespoon chopped cilantro
1 tablespoon chopped sweet red pepper
4 tablespoons grated Cheddar cheese
2 cups shredded lettuce
4 tablespoons Guacamole (see page 14)
   or 1 large avocado, sliced and dipped in
   lemon juice
Dairy sour cream

PREPARATION:

Preheat the oven to broil.

In a skillet, heat the fat and cook the tortillas for about 1 minute or until they are crisp. Drain on paper towels. Spread each tortilla with ¼ cup of the beans, then top with chopped tomatoes, cilantro, sweet pepper and sprinkle the cheese on top.

Broil with tops 2 to 3 inches from the heat, until the cheese is melted, about 3 minutes. Top each with a ½ cup of lettuce and Guacamole (or avocado slices that have been dipped in lemon juice) and a dollop of sour cream.

4 Servings.

Chalupas.

106 TACOS CON JAMÓN Y QUESO

Hold on to your sombreros! The sauce is hot.

RED ENCHILADA SAUCE:

INGREDIENTS:

¼ cup chopped onion
2 tablespoons vegetable oil
3 tablespoons all-purpose flour
1 tablespoon chili powder
½ cup tomato purée
1 clove garlic, crushed
Pinch of oregano
Salt and pepper to taste
1 cup beef stock

PREPARATION:

Sauté the onion in oil until it is transparent. Blend flour, chili powder and tomato purée; stir. Add the garlic, seasonings and beef stock.

Cook until the liquid is reduced to half. Set aside.

Makes about 1 cup of sauce.

TACOS:

INGREDIENTS:

4 tablespoons vegetable oil
4 corn tortillas
1 small onion, chopped
5 tablespoons chopped ham
½ cup Red Enchilada Sauce
1 cup shredded lettuce
4 tablespoons shredded Cheddar or Monterey Jack cheese

PREPARATION:

In a heavy skillet, heat the oil. Warm the tortillas in the oil until they are soft, about 30 seconds. Drain them on paper towels.

Sauté the onion in the oil, add the ham and the sauce. Simmer until the mixture is thick. Spoon 2 tablespoons onto each tortilla slightly below the center. Fold the tortilla in half and fry each taco until it is light golden brown, turning once, about 2 minutes. Drain them on paper towels.

Garnish the tacos with lettuce and cheese.

4 Servings.

ENCHILADAS

A Mexican dinner, or comida, *can consist of as many as six courses—not as great an amount of food as it sounds, because the servings are small. These enchiladas could be any one of them, or just a snack between meals.*

INGREDIENTS:

2 whole green chili peppers, peeled and chopped
1 teaspoon chopped cilantro
1 cup water
1 pound ripe, plum tomatoes, quartered
½ cup chopped onion
2 cloves garlic, peeled
Salt and pepper
2 eggs
¾ cup heavy cream
12 ounces ground beef
1 cup shredded Monterey Jack cheese
¼ cup vegetable oil
8 corn or flour tortillas

PREPARATION:

In a blender or food processor at medium speed, blend chili peppers, cilantro, water, tomatoes and seasoning until smooth. Add eggs and cream and blend into the mixture.

107

In a large skillet, brown the ground beef; add ¼ cup of cold sauce from the blender and half of the cheese.

In a small skillet, heat the vegetable oil and dip tortillas in it until they are soft. Then dip the tortillas in the remainder of the sauce. Place 2 generous tablespoons of the meat on each, roll them up, and arrange them in a baking dish. Pour sauce over the top; sprinkle with remaining cheese.

Bake in the oven for 15 minutes at 350 degrees.

8 Servings.

MOUSSAKA

This is a frequently requested recipe. It is an aromatic Greek stew topped with a light custard.

INGREDIENTS:

**3 large onions, sliced
1 cup olive oil
1 pound minced meat (beef or lamb)
1 cup Fresh Tomato Sauce (see page 77)
½ teaspoon dry herbs
2 large seedless eggplants, sliced
1 cup milk
Salt and pepper to taste
Pinch of nutmeg
3 egg yolks**

PREPARATION:

Preheat the oven to 350 degrees.

In a medium skillet, sauté the onions in ¼ cup of the oil until they are transparent, then add meat and brown. Combine Tomato Sauce with herbs and stir into the meat mixture.

In a separate skillet, heat the remaining olive oil and brown the eggplant slices on each side.

Cover the bottom of a greased, 2½-quart baking dish with the eggplant slices. Spread a layer of the meat mixture over the top, and alternate layers of eggplant and meat until the pan is almost full.

At this point, scald the milk with salt and nutmeg in a saucepan. In a small mixing bowl, beat the egg yolks. Add the eggs to the saucepan and cook the sauce, stirring, over medium heat, until it thickens. Pour this custard-like mixture over the baking dish ingredients, and bake for 45 minutes.

To serve, use a spatula to divide the moussaka among the dinner plates.

4 Servings.

SAVORY CABBAGE ROLLS

The cook's job is made easy with a food processor's help. All the chopping for the stuffing is done quickly.

INGREDIENTS:

**8 tender cabbage leaves
¾ pound ground veal
½ pound chopped sausage
2 slices bacon, chopped
2 tablespoons grated Cheddar cheese
1 egg white
2 tablespoons chopped mushrooms
2 scallions, finely minced
2 cloves garlic, minced
1 tablespoon chopped cilantro
1 teaspoon kummel seeds (caraway)
Pinch of nutmeg
Salt and pepper to taste
4 teaspoons butter or margarine
½ cup thin Tomato Sauce (see page 36)**

PREPARATION:

Preheat the oven to 375 degrees.

To prepare the cabbage leaves: Cut deeply around the stem of the cabbage head to separate the leaves from the core. Dip into boiling water

Savory Cabbage Rolls.

and remove 2 or 3 cabbage leaves. Repeat, dipping the head into the boiling water until eight leaves are removed. Then, blanch the leaves until they are tender, about 2 minutes, and drain. Set aside to cool.

Combine the ground veal, sausage, bacon, cheese, egg white, mushrooms, scallions, garlic, cilantro, kummel seeds, and seasonings. Thoroughly mix together and form into 8 oblong patties.

Wrap a cabbage leaf around each veal patty and secure the roll with a toothpick.

Place the rolls in a greased baking dish and place ½ teaspoon of butter on each roll. Pour Tomato Sauce over them and cover the dish.

Bake in the oven for 35 to 40 minutes, until the meat is cooked through.

CHEF'S TIP:

Use Porcini mushrooms if you can. They are large and round with a brown cap up to 6 inches across. Available in the U.S. in late summer and fall, they are usually imported from France or Italy, fresh or dried.

4 Servings.

NASI GORENG

110

Here is an Indonesian dish with beef and shrimp. A typical example of Southeast Asian cooking which often calls for peanut butter.

INGREDIENTS:

1 cup rice
1 tablespoon margarine or ghee
1 tablespoon lemon juice
2 whole cloves
Salt to taste
1¾ cups cold water
3 tablespoons peanut oil
1 onion, cut into cubes
1 pound top sirloin, cut in small cubes
2 red bell peppers, seeded, ribs removed, cubed
2 tablespoons soy sauce
2 tablespoons peanut butter
12 medium-sized shrimp, shelled and deveined
1 banana, half ripe, peeled and sliced
1 can (6-ounce) Shrimp Chips*

PREPARATION:

To steam rice, combine rice, margarine, lemon juice, cloves, salt and water in a medium saucepan. Water should be cold. Cover and cook at low heat without stirring for 25 minutes or until the liquid is completely evaporated.

In a medium-sized skillet, heat the peanut oil and sauté the onion until it is soft. Reduce the heat, stir in the beef, and cook for 10 minutes. Raise the heat to medium, add the bell pepper, soy sauce, and peanut butter. Cover and cook for 10 minutes.

In a separate skillet, sauté the shrimp in butter. Set aside and sauté the shrimp chips using this skillet.

To serve, top 1 cup of rice with ½ cup of the meat mixture and 3 shrimp in 4 individual casseroles. Garnish with chips and slices of banana.

---

* Shrimp chips are available at Oriental specialty stores. They are inexpensive, but they must be deep-fried.

4 Servings.

MALAY SATAY

An Indonesian barbecue sauce that is very spicy, so be forewarned.

INGREDIENTS:

12 bamboo skewers
¾ pound lamb or chicken, cut in cubes
1 large onion, cubed
¾ pound lean pork meat, cut in cubes
1 sweet, red bell pepper, cubed
2 tablespoons lemon juice
Salt and pepper
1 tablespoon brown sugar
4 tablespoons peanut oil, divided
1 tablespoon soy sauce
1 small onion, finely chopped
1 tablespoon tamarind water (optional)
1 clove garlic, minced
2 tablespoons peanut butter
½ cup coconut milk
1½ tablespoons ground coriander
1½ tablespoons ground cumin
1½ tablespoons ground fennel seeds
½ teaspoon ground chili
2 cups steamed rice

PREPARATION:

Using bamboo skewers, skewer the cubes of meat, onion and pepper.

In a small bowl, combine the lemon juice, salt and pepper, brown sugar and 2 tablespoons of peanut oil; brush onto the meat. Marinate for 1 hour.

In a separate bowl, combine soy sauce, chopped onion, tamarind water, garlic, peanut butter, coconut milk, the remaining peanut oil and spices; stir well.

Barbecue the skewers slowly over hot coals. Turn often.

Serve the meat on the skewers with the sauce nearby for dipping. Serve with Rice Croquettes (see page 7).

6 Servings.

111

Malay Satay.

112

BANANE BEIGNETS AU CURAÇAO LIQUEUR SAUCE

(BANANA FRITTERS IN CURAÇAO LIQUEUR SAUCE)

In addition to their role as desserts, these banana fritters are often served with meat and fish courses (without the Curaçao Liqueur Sauce).

INGREDIENTS:

4 bananas, half ripe
1 tablespoon brown sugar
½ teaspoon lime juice
2 ounces brandy or rum
⅓ cup all-purpose flour
½ cup milk
1 egg, whole
½ teaspoon baking powder
1 cup corn or soya bean oil
Curaçao Liqueur Sauce

PREPARATION:

Cut each banana into 3 pieces and marinate in a mixture of sugar, lime juice and brandy for 2 hours; drain.

To prepare the batter, combine flour and milk, in a 2-quart bowl. Blend until smooth; add egg and baking powder. Then add bananas to the batter, coating them well.

In a deep skillet, heat the oil, then drop the coated pieces in and sauté them for about 5 to 6 minutes, or until they are golden brown.

Serve with Curaçao Liqueur Sauce.

4 Servings.

CURAÇAO LIQUEUR SAUCE:

Flavored with brandy, this sauce is one of those used for the traditional steamed Christmas pudding.

INGREDIENTS:

6 tablespoons butter
⅔ cup confectioners sugar
2 egg yolks
¾ cup heavy cream
3 tablespoons Curaçao liqueur

PREPARATION:

Cream the butter with the sugar until the mixture is light and fluffy. Beat in the egg yolks, one at a time. Pour the mixture into a saucepan and stir in the cream. Cook over medium-low heat, stirring constantly, until the mixture coats a wooden spoon. Remove it from the heat and pour it into a serving bowl. Flavor it with the liqueur.

Makes 2 cups.

BLUEBERRY CRUMB MUFFINS

These muffins, alone or with a scoop of vanilla ice cream are a special treat.

INGREDIENTS:

2 cups all-purpose flour
¼ cup granulated sugar
1 tablespoon baking powder
1½ teaspoons salt
¼ teaspoon ground nutmeg
1 egg
1 cup milk
3 tablespoons butter or margarine, melted
1 cup blueberries

PREPARATION:

Preheat oven to 400 degrees. Grease 2½-inch muffin tins.

In a large bowl, stir together flour, sugar, baking powder, salt and nutmeg.

In a medium bowl, beat egg with milk and melted butter. Add egg mixture to flour mixture, stirring just until dry ingredients are moistened. Stir in blueberries with last few strokes.

Fill prepared muffin pans about ¾ full. Sprinkle tops evenly with Butter Crumb Topping. Bake for 25 to 30 minutes until well browned. Serve warm.

Makes 12 muffins.

BUTTER CRUMB TOPPING:

INGREDIENTS:

⅓ cup all-purpose flour
⅓ cup granulated sugar
¼ teaspoon ground cinnamon
¼ cup cold butter or margarine

PREPARATION:

In a small bowl, mix flour, sugar and cinnamon. Cut in cold butter until coarse crumbs form.

Blueberry Crumb Muffins.

113

114   CINNAMON SCONES

Scones are short biscuits often served at teatime.

INGREDIENTS:

2 cups all-purpose flour
2 teaspoons baking powder
½ teaspoon baking soda
½ teaspoon salt
½ cup butter or margarine
1 egg, separated
3 tablespoons honey
⅓ cup buttermilk
1 tablespoon granulated sugar
¼ teaspoon ground cinnamon

PREPARATION:

Preheat the oven to 400 degrees.

In a large bowl, stir together flour, baking powder, baking soda and salt. Cut in butter until the mixture is the consistency of coarse crumbs.

In a small bowl, beat egg yolk (reserving the white) with honey and buttermilk until blended. Add the buttermilk mixture to the flour mixture, stirring lightly only until dough clings together.

Using floured hands, lightly shape dough into a flattened ball. Roll or pat out on a floured board or pastry cloth to a circle about ½-inch thick and 8½ inches in diameter. Using a floured knife, cut 8 or 12 equal wedges. Place them slightly apart on a greased or non-stick baking sheet.

In a small bowl, beat egg white slightly — to a froth.

In another bowl, blend 1 tablespoon sugar and cinnamon. Brush scones lightly with egg white, then sprinkle them with the cinnamon and sugar mixture.

Bake for 10 to 12 minutes, or until golden brown. Serve warm.

Makes 8 to 12 scones.

Opposite page: Cherries Jubilee, recipe on page 117.

DESSERTS

116

Banane Flambé au Curaçao
Cherries Jubilee
Crêpes Suzette
Rice Torta
Napolitan Cassata
Fruitcake
Sacher Torte
Viennese Chocolate Torte
Mango and Pineapple Cake
Charlotte Mould
Crème Brûlée
Fried Vanilla Custard
Zabaglione with Blackberries
Pavlova
Floating Islands
Chocolate Orange Mousse
Lemon Soufflé
Soufflé au Chocolat et au Sauce Grand Marnier
Chilled Strawberry Soufflé
Biscuit Tortoni
Bread Pudding with Rum Sauce
Martinique Fruit Cocktail
Rum Sherbet, Homemade
Crusty Apple Pie
Tarte aux Fraises

A detail from the Tarte aux Fraises, recipe on page 136.

BANANE FLAMBÉ AU CURAÇAO

This flaming banana dessert has a Caribbean flavor — a warming conclusion for a winter meal.

INGREDIENTS:

5 tablespoons sweet butter
6 large half-ripe bananas, peeled and cut in
half lengthwise
2 tablespoons all-purpose flour
Juice of 4 oranges
Peel of 1 orange
6 tablespoons granulated sugar
1 cinnamon stick
2 cloves
3 ounces Curaçao liqueur
2 ounces vodka
Whipped cream or vanilla ice cream
Flaked coconut (optional)

PREPARATION:

In a large skillet, melt the butter and sauté the bananas, sprinkled with flour, for 2 minutes on each side. Add the orange juice and peel, sugar, cinnamon stick and cloves. Boil for 4 more minutes or until the liquid is reduced by half. Remove the orange peel, cinnamon and cloves.

Add the liqueur and vodka to the pan. Ignite it, and shake the pan until the flame dies. Stir to blend the sauce.

Serve the bananas immediately, topped with whipped cream or ice cream and sprinkle with coconut, if you like.

CHEF'S TIP:

Warm Curaçao liqueur and vodka first before adding to the sauce; they will ignite better.

6 Servings.

CHERRIES JUBILEE

The excitement of having a flambéed fruit dish prepared at the table, makes Cherries Jubilee a popular festive dessert in Princess Cruises' dining rooms.

INGREDIENTS:

¼ cup granulated sugar
¼ cup orange juice
2 tablespoons lemon juice
1 cup Bing cherries, pitted and drained
1 ounce maraschino cherry juice
2 ounces Cherry Heering or kirsch
4 large scoops vanilla ice cream
½ cup whipped heavy cream
4 tablespoons chopped almonds

PREPARATION:

In a saucepan over medium heat, combine the sugar, orange and lemon juices, stirring well until the sugar dissolves. Add the cherries and maraschino juice, and cook over high heat for 5 minutes. Warm the liqueur, ignite and pour it over the cherries.

Serve in 4 individual dishes over a scoop of vanilla ice cream. Top with whipped cream and sprinkle with chopped almonds.

4 Servings.

118
CRÊPES SUZETTE

You can prepare this flaming crêpe dessert at the table in a chafing dish, or assemble it in the kitchen and flame it at the table.

CRÊPES:

INGREDIENTS:

¼ cup all-purpose flour, sifted
1 tablespoon confectioners sugar
Pinch of salt
2 whole eggs
2 egg yolks
⅓ teaspoon vanilla extract
⅓ teaspoon orange rind, grated
1 cup milk
1 teaspoon melted butter

PREPARATION:

To prepare the batter: Into a large mixing bowl, sift together the flour, sugar and salt. In another small bowl, beat the eggs and yolks; add vanilla and orange rind. While stirring, add the milk, alternately with the eggs, to the flour. Beat until smooth. Refrigerate for at least 1 hour.

Coat the bottom of a heavy 7-inch skillet with butter. Ladle in 2 tablespoons of batter, and tilt the pan so as to cover the entire bottom with a thin layer of batter. Brown both sides lightly. Remove from the skillet and stack on a platter with paper towels between them. Repeat until the batter is used up.

Makes approximately 10 to 12.

CRÊPES SUZETTE SAUCE:

INGREDIENTS:

2 orange rinds
1 lemon rind
6 sugar lumps
4 tablespoons granulated sugar
3 tablespoons sweet butter
Juice of 2 large oranges, freshly squeezed and
   strained
¼ cup Grand Marnier liqueur
½ lemon
2 ounces Cognac for flambéing

PREPARATION:

Cut the orange and lemon rinds into thin strips. Rub the sugar lumps into one of the orange rinds for the oil of the fruit to penetrate the sugar. Place the granulated sugar in a cook-and-serve skillet, and stir over low heat until it is brown. Add the sugar lumps and butter. Stir until the lumps are melted. Add the orange juice, sugared rind and liqueur; simmer for 5 minutes.

To serve, heat the sauce over medium heat. Place each crêpe in the pan individually, coating each side with the sauce. Then, fold each crêpe twice, into fourths; it should resemble a triangle. When the crêpes are arranged in the skillet, squeeze the lemon over them, and raise the heat until very hot. Pour the Cognac over the crêpes and ignite the sauce with a long tapered match. Serve while still alight with a spoon, pouring extra sauce over each crêpe as you serve.

Serve in warmed dishes. Pour remaining juice over crêpes.

Makes about 1 cup.

Crêpes Suzette.

RICE TORTA

This dish comes from the area near Genoa called the Italian Riviera where each family prides itself on having the original recipe — and the best.

INGREDIENTS:

2 quarts water
½ cup uncooked Arborio rice
Zest of 1 lemon
1 stick cinnamon
4 eggs
¾ cup granulated sugar
1 teaspoon grated lemon rind
1 ounce cherry brandy (kirsch)
½ cup milk
3 tablespoons butter, melted
½ teaspoon salt

PREPARATION:

Preheat the oven to 375 degrees.

In a large saucepan, bring salted water to a boil, add rice, lemon zest and cinnamon stick. Simmer for 35 minutes; drain well. Remove the lemon and cinnamon and let the rice cool.

In a medium-sized bowl, combine the eggs, sugar, grated lemon rind and cherry brandy. Mix well until it is foamy. Add the milk, boiled rice and butter.

Pour the mixture into a greased 9-inch baking pan. Bake for 1 hour. The top should be a golden brown, but not too dark. The cake has the consistency of a pudding.

Makes 1 (9-inch) cake.

NAPOLITAN CASSATA

Cassata is a layer cake with filling. It was once served only at such feasts of renewal as Christmas and Easter. Today, it is often served at weddings, to signify the beginning of a new way of life.

INGREDIENTS:

1 pound cake (12-ounces), baked and ready to frost
4 ounces semi-sweet chocolate
½ cup sweet butter
⅓ cup brewed espresso coffee
1 pound ricotta cheese
⅓ cup granulated sugar
¼ cup mixed candied citrus peel
¼ cup semi-sweet chocolate shavings
2 ounces Triple Sec liqueur

PREPARATION:

Bake or buy the pound cake — about 9 inches long and 3 inches wide. With a sharp, serrated knife, cut the cake twice, making 3 lengthwise layers.

To make the frosting: Melt the 4 ounces of semi-sweet chocolate and the butter together in the top of a double boiler over simmering water. Stir to mix and then whisk in the espresso. Remove the chocolate mixture from the heat and place it in the refrigerator. Stir every 15 minutes until it is smooth and firm.

To make the filling: Mix together the ricotta, sugar and candied citrus peels. Beat until smooth, then fold in the chocolate shavings.

Sprinkle half of the liqueur on the bottom layer. Spread half of the ricotta mixture on the pound cake. Top with the second layer

Napolitan Cassata.

and repeat the process. Top with the third and final layer.

Cover the entire cake with ¼ inch of frosting. To do this, use a narrow cake spatula dipped occasionally in hot water. Use a pastry tube to decorate the cake with colored frosting buds and floral vines.

8 Servings.

FRUITCAKE

Winter holiday guests will enjoy this fruitcake. It improves with age, so it should be baked weeks in advance.

INGREDIENTS:

1½ cups raisins
⅓ cup rum
1 cup plus 2 tablespoons butter
2¼ cups confectioners sugar
4 eggs, separated
1¾ cups all-purpose flour
1 teaspoon baking powder
½ teaspoon salt
1 cup chopped candied fruit

PREPARATION:

Preheat the oven to 350 degrees.

Soak the raisins in rum for about 30 minutes.

In a large mixing bowl, cream the butter until it is light and smooth. Beat in confectioners sugar, a little at a time. Beat egg whites to stiff peaks. Stir half of the beaten egg whites into the butter mixture. Then gently fold in the remaining whites. Add egg yolks, blending well. Stir the flour, baking powder and salt into the mixture. Allow the mixture to rest.

Stir soaked raisins and any remaining rum and candied fruit into the cake batter.

Butter a 9-inch loaf pan and line the bottom neatly with wax paper. Butter the paper. Pour batter into the prepared pan. Smooth the surface with a spatula.

Bake for 1 hour or until the cake tests done. Cool on a wire rack. Slice to serve.

CHEF'S TIP:

If the fruitcake becomes dry, sprinkle the top lightly with rum. Wrap it tightly in a cloth or plastic wrap, and let it stand until it is moistened throughout. Repeat as desired.

Makes 1 (9-inch) cake.

SACHER TORTE

A well-known Viennese dense chocolate cake with apricot filling.

INGREDIENTS:

6 tablespoons sweet butter
3 tablespoons granulated sugar
3 squares semi-sweet chocolate
1 teaspoon vanilla extract
4 egg yolks
¾ cup cake flour
3 egg whites, stiffly beaten
½ cup apricot jam
½ cup chocolate icing

PREPARATION:

Preheat the oven to 350 degrees. Grease and flour a 9-inch cake pan.

In a large bowl, cream the butter, add the sugar gradually and beat together until light and fluffy. Gradually add the melted chocolate and vanilla. Add the egg yolks, one at a time, mix well after each addition. Fold in the flour and the egg whites.

Turn the batter into the prepared pan and bake in a pre-heated oven for about 20 minutes at 350 degrees, or until a cake tester inserted into the center comes out clean. Let cake stand for 10 to 15 minutes on a cooling rack before turning it out of the pan onto a wire rack to cool completely.

Cut the cake in 2 parts and place 1 layer, rounded-side down on a cake platter; spread evenly with the jam as you would a sandwich. Place the second layer, rounded-side up, over the filled layer. With a spatula, cover the top and sides with chocolate icing. The cake should be refrigerated until you are ready to serve.

Chocolate Icing: In a double boiler over boiling water, melt 2 ounces of unsweetened chocolate. Remove from the heat; add ½ cup of confectioners sugar, 1 tablespoon water and 1 egg; mix well. Finally, add 2 tablespoons sweet butter; mix until it is creamy. Pour on the cake and spread to cover.

Makes 1 (9-inch) cake.

Sacher Torte.

124

VIENNESE CHOCOLATE TORTE

A gorgeous, rich chocolate cake that originated in Vienna, once the undisputed capital of confectionary art.

TORTE:

INGREDIENTS:

⅓ cup sweet butter, softened
6 tablespoons all-purpose flour
3 ounces semi-sweet chocolate
½ cup granulated sugar
3 eggs, separated, reserve whites
⅓ cup finely ground walnuts
1 cup canned, pitted tart red cherries, drained

PREPARATION:

Preheat the oven to 350 degrees.

Using ½ tablespoon of butter and 1 tablespoon of flour, lightly grease and flour a 9-inch springform pan; tap out excess flour and set the pan aside.

In a double boiler, melt the chocolate over boiling water; cool to room temperature.

Meanwhile, in a large bowl, beat the remaining butter until creamy. Gradually beat in the sugar until the mixture is light and fluffy. Beat in the melted chocolate and the egg yolks, one at a time.

In a small bowl, combine walnuts and the remaining flour.

In a separate bowl, beat the egg whites until stiff but not dry. Gently fold the egg whites by thirds into the chocolate mixture alternately with thirds of the walnut mixture. Spoon the mixture into the prepared pan and shake it until it is evenly distributed. Pat the cherries dry with paper towels and scatter them evenly over the batter.

Bake for 1 hour or until a cake tester inserted into the center comes out clean. Cool the torte and then remove it from the baking pan.

MOCHA GLAZE:

INGREDIENTS:

6 ounces semi-sweet chocolate
¼ cup strongly brewed coffee

PREPARATION:

Stir chocolate and coffee in the top portion of a double boiler over boiling water until it is melted. Then spread the glaze over the top and sides of the torte.

Chill until the glaze has set before serving.

Makes 1 (9-inch) torte.

MANGO AND PINEAPPLE CAKE

A luscious cake covered with sparkling, glazed pineapple. An ideal choice for a Mexican dinner.

INGREDIENTS:

½ cup custard cream
1 orange sponge cake (9-inch diameter, ¾-inch thick)
1 puff pastry disc (9-inch diameter, ¼-inch thick)
½ cup mango pulp
3 tablespoons brown sugar
3 tablespoons orange juice
½ pound pineapple, thinly sliced
1 ounce Kahlua liqueur
8 maraschino cherries

PREPARATION:

To prepare the custard cream: Use 2 or 3 egg yolks to 1 cup of heavy cream. Beat together. Heat carefully, but do not allow to boil.

Pour the custard cream over the sponge cake. Use a spatula to cover it well. Top with puff pastry. Pour mango pulp and spread to cover the pastry well.

In a skillet at medium temperature, melt the sugar until it is caramelized and add the orange juice. Reduce the liquid until the mixture turns golden and thick. Sauté the pineapple for 2 minutes. Let the pineapple cool and combine the slices to cover the mango pulp. Garnish with cherries.

8 Servings. Makes 1 (9-inch)cake.

CHARLOTTE MOULD

(DANISH LEMON "FROMAGE")

A delicate lemon flavor graces this feather-light dessert.

INGREDIENTS:

Juice of 1 lemon
1 teaspoon lemon rind, grated
½ teaspoon almond extract
2 tablespoons unflavored gelatin
6 egg whites
5 tablespoons confectioners sugar
1½ cups heavy cream, whipped
Fresh berries

PREPARATION:

Combine lemon juice, rind and almond extract. Sprinkle gelatin over this mixture and let it stand until gelatin is completely dissolved.

In a medium-sized bowl, using an electric mixer, beat egg whites and confectioners sugar until soft peaks form.

Fold the whipped cream into the beaten egg whites; gently fold in the gelatin mixture. Spoon the mixture into a 7-inch charlotte mold or a bowl and chill until set (about 6 hours).

To serve, turn the mold onto a serving platter, and surround it with fresh berries.

8 Servings.

126   CRÈME BRÛLÉE

A chilled caramel custard staple of the dessert table.

INGREDIENTS:

2 tablespoons brown sugar
2 cups light cream
6 tablespoons granulated sugar
1 vanilla pod
4 egg yolks
1 teaspoon cornstarch or 1 tablespoon
    white flour

PREPARATION:

In a pudding mold, caramelize the brown sugar over high heat until it is dark brown.

In a medium-sized saucepan, heat the cream, sugar and vanilla pod.

In the bowl of an electric mixer, beat the egg yolks until they are thickened. Add the cornstarch, and blend well. Remove the pod from the cream mixture, and add a small amount (about ¼ cup) to the egg mixture, beating constantly. Now, add the egg mixture to the cream mixture, mixing thoroughly. Continue to cook, stirring constantly, until the custard coats the spoon. Pour the mixture into the prepared mold and place it in the refrigerator to chill.

To serve, run a thin knife between the custard and the mold and turn onto a dessert plate. The caramelized sugar should run down the sides.

Serve with lady fingers, berries or cream.

4 Servings.

FRIED VANILLA CUSTARD

Individual custard cakes served warm.

INGREDIENTS:

3 eggs, separated
4 tablespoons granulated sugar
2 tablespoons all-purpose flour
1 cup milk
Zest of 1 lemon
⅓ vanilla pod
½ cup plain bread crumbs
1 cup cooking oil
1 tablespoon confectioners sugar

PREPARATION:

Mix egg yolks with sugar, and beat until they are pale in color. Add the flour and stir well.

In a small saucepan, scald milk, lemon zest and vanilla and pour it into the egg mixture. Stir and cook for 5 minutes. Remove lemon and vanilla. Pour the cream into a small baking pan (6-inches long by 2-inches wide) and let it cool. Cut into 4 pieces.

Beat the egg whites until they are stiff. Dip each custard cake in the egg white and then roll it in bread crumbs to coat.

In a deep skillet, heat the oil and fry the custards until they are golden.

Sprinkle with confectioners sugar, and serve them warm.

4 Servings.

ZABAGLIONE WITH BLACKBERRIES

One of our chefs' most popular specialties.

INGREDIENTS:

1 cup blackberries
6 tablespoons granulated sugar
2 tablespoons orange juice
4 egg yolks
½ cup Marsala wine
4 Amaretto biscuits

PREPARATION:

In a small bowl, combine blackberries, 2 tablespoons of the sugar and orange juice; set aside for 1 hour.

In the top of a double boiler or *bain marie,* over simmering water, combine egg yolks with 4 tablespoons sugar. Beat with an electric mixer or rotary beater until it is pale and fluffy. Gradually add the Marsala wine, and beat until the zabaglione is thick enough to hold its shape in a spoon. The process can take up to 10 minutes. Be careful not to overcook it; remove from heat.

Divide the berries into 4 champagne saucers, pour in the zabaglione. Garnish with Amaretto biscuits.

Serve hot or chilled.

CHEF'S TIP:

The water in the bottom pan of the double boiler must be boiling before you pour the egg mixture into the top pan!

4 Servings.

Zabaglione with Blackberries.

128 PAVLOVA

Named after the famous ballerina, this graceful dessert resembles the skirt of a tutu. It is very delicate, and should be served immediately after it is done.

INGREDIENTS:

3 egg whites
Pinch of salt
2 tablespoons white vinegar
½ teaspoon vanilla extract
4 tablespoons brown sugar
1 tablespoon potato starch
Passion fruit pulp, kiwi slices, or strawberries
1 cup whipped cream

PREPARATION:

Preheat the oven to 300 degrees. Grease and flour a 9-inch cake pan.

Beat the egg whites and salt into peaks.

In a separate bowl, mix together vinegar, vanilla and sugar. Slowly stir in potato starch. Gently fold the egg whites into the mixture using a wooden spoon; do not stir. Transfer the mixture into the prepared baking pan.

Bake in the preheated oven until the meringue is firm and crisp — about 1 hour.

Spread the top with slightly sweetened whipped cream, and garnish with passion fruit pulp for a *real* Pavlova. (Other fruits may be substituted.)

Makes 1 (9-inch) cake.

Floating Islands.

FLOATING ISLANDS

These meringues are so pretty in a chocolate sauce.

INGREDIENTS:

3 large eggs, separated
¾ cup granulated sugar
2 cups milk
Zest of lemon (optional)
Pinch of cinnamon
Pinch of nutmeg
Dash of vanilla extract
1 tablespoon all-purpose flour
3 ounces unsweetened chocolate, melted
**Whipped cream and maraschino cherries for
   garnish (optional)**

PREPARATION:

Beat egg whites until foamy. Gradually add ½ cup of the sugar; beat until egg whites turn stiff.

In a skillet, scald the milk and lower the heat to simmer. Divide meringue into 8 oblong parts, and drop them into the milk, one at a time, and simmer for 8 minutes. Do not turn the meringues over. With a slotted spoon, lift them out to a plate and allow them to cool. Remove the skillet from the heat, but keep the milk warm over a pan of warm water.

To make the sauce: In a medium-sized bowl, combine egg yolks, remaining sugar, lemon zest, cinnamon, nutmeg and vanilla. Add the flour and stir until the mixture is smooth. Add melted chocolate diluted in the reserved milk. Bring the mixture to a boil. Pour it into a dessert dish and chill.

Before serving, top the chocolate mixture with floating meringues. Garnish each with a pom-pom of whipped cream and a maraschino cherry (optional).

4 Servings.

130 CHOCOLATE ORANGE MOUSSE

This mousse is a richly satisfying dessert. Chocolate and orange are a delicious combination.

INGREDIENTS:

½ cup orange juice
1 teaspoon orange rind, grated
3 tablespoons unflavored gelatin
2 eggs
½ cup granulated sugar
½ cup water
6 ounces Dutch dark semi-sweet chocolate
1 ounce Cointreau liqueur
1 cup heavy cream, whipped

PREPARATION:

Combine the orange juice and rind. Sprinkle gelatin over the juice and let it soften for 5 minutes. Stir until gelatin is completely dissolved.

In a medium-sized mixing bowl using an electric mixer, beat eggs and sugar until thickened, about 3 minutes.

Combine water and chocolate in the top of double boiler. Heat until chocolate is completely melted. Remove from heat and add liqueur. Cool thoroughly.

In a large mixing bowl, thoroughly combine the gelatin with the eggs and the melted chocolate mixtures. Gently fold in whipping cream. Spoon into 6 individual bowls or champagne glasses and chill until set.

6 Servings.

LEMON SOUFFLÉ

This is a different recipe for a fast soufflé.

INGREDIENTS:

1 tablespoon grated lemon rind
3 egg yolks
1 teaspoon vanilla extract
2 tablespoons all-purpose flour
4 egg whites
Pinch of salt
4 tablespoons granulated sugar
Confectioners sugar

PREPARATION:

Preheat the oven to 350 degrees. Butter a 1½-quart soufflé dish.

In a mixing bowl, combine lemon rind, egg yolks and vanilla; mix and gradually add the flour; mix well for 2 minutes. In a separate bowl, combine the egg whites and salt; beat until the whites are frothy. Slowly add 3 tablespoons of the sugar and beat until the whites are stiff but not dry.

Fold the egg whites into the egg yolk mixture. Pour into the prepared soufflé dish and sprinkle with remaining sugar. Bake for 12 minutes or until soufflé is puffed and lightly browned. Dust confectioners sugar over the top.

Serve the soufflé hot or chilled, with a sauce to your taste.

4 Servings.

Lemon Soufflé.

132 SOUFFLÉ AU CHOCOLAT ET AU SAUCE GRAND MARNIER

(CHOCOLATE SOUFFLÉ WITH GRAND MARNIER SAUCE)

Soufflé for dessert makes even the most ordinary dinner special.

INGREDIENTS:

3 tablespoons butter
2 tablespoons all-purpose flour
1 cup milk
2 ounces (2 squares) unsweetened chocolate
½ cup granulated sugar
1 teaspoon vanilla extract
4 egg yolks
5 egg whites, at room temperature
Confectioners sugar
2 cups Grand Marnier Sauce

PREPARATION:

Preheat the oven to 400 degrees. Grease the bottom and sides of a 7-inch diameter soufflé pan and dust with sugar. Then, turn the pan upside down to shake out excess sugar.

Make a *roux* with butter and flour; cook and stir them together over moderate heat until you have a smooth paste. Gradually add milk; stir and cook until the mixture thickens. Add chocolate and sugar, and stir until chocolate is melted. Cool before adding vanilla and egg yolks.

In a separate 2-quart bowl, beat the egg whites until stiff peaks form, then, gently and lightly, fold them into the chocolate mixture. Pour into the prepared soufflé dish.

Place the dish in a pan half filled with warm water and bake in the preheated oven for 15 minutes. Reduce heat to 350 degrees and bake for another 20 minutes. Sift confectioners sugar over the top. Serve immediately with brandy or custard sauce, or another sauce to your taste.

4 Servings.

GRAND MARNIER SAUCE:

INGREDIENTS:

6 egg yolks
1 teaspoon vanilla extract
¼ teaspoon ground nutmeg
⅓ cup granulated sugar
⅓ cup heavy cream
½ cup half-and-half
4 tablespoons Grand Marnier liqueur
½ teaspoon grated orange zest (orange portion of peel)

PREPARATION:

Beat the egg yolks, vanilla, nutmeg and sugar with a whisk in a medium saucepan until light in color, about 5 minutes.

Scald heavy cream and half-and-half in a separate saucepan. Stir the hot cream slowly into the egg yolks. Using low heat and stirring constantly, cook until sauce thickens and coats a wooden spoon; do not allow it to boil. Remove from heat and pour the sauce into a cold container to prevent further cooking.

Stir in Grand Marnier and orange zest. Cool to room temperature. Refrigerate before serving.

Makes about 2 cups.

CHILLED STRAWBERRY SOUFFLÉ

This soufflé can be made with any kind of berry — raspberries, blueberries or blackberries.

INGREDIENTS:

1 cup heavy cream
Dash of vanilla extract
2 tablespoons confectioners sugar
2 tablespoons Cointreau liqueur
1 cup granulated sugar
1 cup crushed strawberries

PREPARATION:

Beat the heavy cream with vanilla and confectioners sugar, until stiff.

In a bowl combine the Cointreau, granulated sugar and strawberries. Fold in the cream mixture.

Pour into 4 individual soufflé dishes and place them in the freezer for several hours.

Garnish with orange segments or whole berries and sweetened whipped cream

4 Servings.

BISCUIT TORTONI

Created long ago by an Italian ice cream vendor named Tortoni, Biscuit Tortoni is still the sweet crowning achievement of southern Italian meals.

INGREDIENTS:

½ cup heavy cream
6 tablespoons confectioners sugar
1 egg white
¼ teaspoon cream of tartar
½ cup crumbled amaretti cookies (crumbs)
1 tablespoon sherry, sweet
Maraschino cherries for garnish (optional)

PREPARATION:

In a small bowl, whip the cream with sugar until stiff.

In a separate bowl, combine egg white and cream of tartar; beat until stiff peaks form. Fold the egg white and part of the amaretti crumbs into the whipped cream; add the sherry and then spoon into 4 paper cups. Sprinkle with remaining amaretti crumbs and refrigerate.

Serve garnished with maraschino cherries.

4 Servings.

134 BREAD PUDDING WITH RUM SAUCE

A good old Yankee dish, still featured in many of the best hotels.

INGREDIENTS:

6 slices white bread, cut into cubes
2 cups half-and-half
5 tablespoons butter
3 eggs, beaten
1 cup granulated sugar
1 Granny Smith apple, peeled and diced
6 ounces dried apricots, chopped
4 tablespoons golden raisins
4 tablespoons chopped walnuts
1 ounce brandy
1 tablespoon combined spices (1 teaspoon
   each nutmeg, cinnamon, allspice)
1 teaspoon vanilla extract
¼ teaspoon salt

PREPARATION:

Preheat the oven to 350 degrees.

Place the bread cubes in a bowl. In a saucepan, combine the half-and-half and 4 tablespoons of butter; heat until the butter is melted. Pour over the bread cubes. Let stand for 10 minutes. Then add beaten eggs and the remaining ingredients.

With the remaining tablespoon of butter, grease a 6- by 5-inch pudding mold and dust with flour.

Pour the pudding mixture into the prepared mold. Cover tightly and bake for 45 minutes.

Serve warm with rum sauce.

RUM SAUCE:

INGREDIENTS:

1 cup granulated sugar
2 tablespoons cornstarch
1⅓ cups water
3 tablespoons rum, or 1¼ teaspoons of rum
   flavoring
3 tablespoons butter

PREPARATION:

In a saucepan, combine sugar and cornstarch, and add the water. Cook and stir until thickened. Cook for 2 minutes more. Remove from heat. Add rum and butter.

6 Servings.

MARTINIQUE FRUIT COCKTAIL

A cooling mix of tropical fruits over rum sherbet.

INGREDIENTS:

Juice of 2 large oranges
4 tablespoons granulated sugar
Dash of salt
1 banana, peeled and sliced into ½-inch
    pieces
1 large ripe mango, peeled and cut into ½-inch
    cubes
½ pound papaya, diced into ½-inch cubes
1 tangelo, segmented
½ pound watermelon flesh, cut into ½-inch
    cubes
8 scoops Rum Sherbet, Homemade (or 1 pint
    lime sherbet and 3 tablespoons white rum)
12 fresh mint leaves

PREPARATION:

In a bowl, mix the orange juice, sugar, and salt. Add the cut fruit directly into the bowl. Mix the fruits in the marinade at least one hour before serving.

Instead of rum sherbet, you may substitute the following: 1 pint lime sherbet and 3 tablespoons white rum. Let the sherbet soften slightly; stir in the rum. Re-freeze the mixture.

Serve the fruit in a cocktail cup topped with a small scoop of sherbet and mint leaves.

8 Servings.

RUM SHERBET, HOMEMADE

INGREDIENTS:

1 pint water
6 tablespoons dark brown sugar
1 cinnamon stick
Peel of 1 lime
Juice of 1 lime
3 ounces rum

PREPARATION:

In a small saucepan, combine water, sugar, cinnamon and lime peel. Bring to a boil for 10 minutes. Strain and allow it to cool. Add lime juice and rum.

Pour the mixture into an ice-cream maker, and allow it to freeze until it is medium-hard, or ready to serve.

Makes 6 scoops of sherbet.

CRUSTY APPLE PIE

It seems that everyone loves apple pie, and every country has one. Princess Cruises' chefs offer this one. Using a sweet pie dough, pâte sucrée, the texture is not flaky or tender but more like a cookie dough. It's delicious.

INGREDIENTS:

1 cup all-purpose flour
8 tablespoons sweet butter, cut up
½ cup granulated sugar
2 egg yolks
½ teaspoon grated lemon rind
2 tablespoons heavy cream
2 tablespoons water
6 tablespoons apricot jam
3 large Granny Smith apples
2 tablespoons dark brown sugar
1 tablespoon brandy

PREPARATION:

Preheat the oven to 350 degrees.

In a large mixing bowl, combine the flour, butter, granulated sugar, egg yolks, lemon rind, and cream, stirring with a fork until the dough is fairly smooth. Knead the dough with your fingertips for a minute and shape it into a ball. Wrap it with plastic wrap. Chill the dough for about 1 hour before using it.

To prepare the crust, roll the dough out on a floured surface to a circle about ⅛-inch thick, and line a buttered 9-inch pie plate with it.

For the glaze, mix together the jam and water in a saucepan. Bring it to a boil and simmer for 3 minutes. Let it cool.

Peel and core the apples. Cut each in half and slice each half into ¼-inch thick slices. Toss the slices in the brown sugar and sprinkle with brandy. Brush the inside bottom of the crust with a thin layer of the glaze. Fill the crust with the apples. Spread the surface of the apple slices with the remaining glaze.

Bake in the preheated oven for 45 minutes.

Makes 1 (9-inch) pie.

TARTE AUX FRAISES

(STRAWBERRY TART)

A typically French finale to the meal, this tart is perfectly lovely, glittering with jam glacé.

INGREDIENTS:

1¼ cups buttermilk baking mix
½ cup granulated sugar
1 tablespoon grated orange peel
¼ cup margarine
1 quart fresh strawberries, rinsed and hulled
1 tablespoon cornstarch
2 tablespoons water
½ cup orange juice
1 tablespoon granulated sugar
½ cup heavy cream, chilled
2 tablespoons granulated sugar

PREPARATION:

Preheat the oven to 400 degrees.

Combine baking mix, ½ cup sugar and orange peel. Cut in margarine until the mixture resembles coarse cornmeal. Press the mixture in

Tarte aux Fraises.

the bottom of an ungreased 9-inch round baking pan. Bake for 10 to 12 minutes or until light brown; cool for about 30 minutes.

Invert crust on a serving plate. Arrange strawberries on the crust. Dissolve cornstarch in water and combine with orange juice and 1 tablespoon of sugar in a small saucepan. Heat to boiling, stirring constantly. Boil and stir for 1 minute, then cool completely. Pour orange glaze over strawberries. Refrigerate for 1 hour.

Whip cream with sugar in a chilled 2-quart bowl until stiff. Using an icing bag, decorate the tart with the whipped cream.

8 Servings.

MEET THE CHEFS

It is in the dining rooms of Princess Cruises where passengers enjoy some of the most memorable highlights of their cruise. Our award-winning chefs and their staff provide superb continental gourmet cuisine for which Princess is famous. We'd like to introduce them to you.

Elio Allegra

Emilio Barucci

Antonio Cereda

Giampaolo Marchi

ELIO ALLEGRA

Born in 1948 at Briga Novarese, a quaint little village at the foot of the Italian Alps, Elio Allegra comes from a family of cooks and chefs.

Following in the footsteps of his father and grandfather, he spent a great deal of his childhood in the kitchen. In 1961, at the age of 13, he started his apprenticeship for what was to be a long and rewarding career at the Grand Hotel Boston of Stresa, one of the most famous ski resorts in the Italian Alps.

After holding a series of positions in prestigious hotels and restaurants, he joined Princess Cruises in 1979 as sous chef, earning the esteem of his supervisors and the respect of the whole galley staff.

In 1984 he was appointed chef de cuisine of the M/V Royal Princess. Moving from one ship to another, he has enriched all of them with his magic touch and cheerful personality.

Chef Allegra and his wife are the parents of a son and a daughter, and they make their home at Briga Novarese.

He is an avid fan of Italian soccer and American football. Milan and the '49ers are the teams he likes the most.

EMILIO BARUCCI

Chef Emilio Barucci was born in 1933 in La Spezia into a family of chefs. His father, Giovanni, was a chef de cuisine, and his grandfather Emilio and uncle Ezio were also chefs.

When he was 16, he began helping his father with his work. Later he attended the Diano Marina School of Cooking and worked in hotels in San Remo as an apprentice.

At 20, Chef Barucci went to sea. Beginning as a crew cook, he worked at all levels, including pastry cook. In 1967, he joined the company as a first chef, and in 1974, he was promoted to executive chef.

One of his best creations remains the Tagliatelle Chef Style.

His hobby is ice carving, and his ice creations beautify the buffet tables of Princess Cruises' ships.

ANTONIO CEREDA

Antonio Cereda, chef of the M/V Royal Princess, was born in the little village of Armeno, in the Piedmont region of Italy not far from Turin, one of the leading Italian industrial centers.

Chef Cereda began his culinary studies at the hotel institute at the famous Italian resort of Stresa. After graduating, he moved to the prestigious Hotel Des Bains in Venezia. Subsequently, he spent several years touring the ski resorts of Northern Italy and Switzerland, refining his skills, and improving his culinary knowledge. He also found time to practice his favorite sport — skiing.

From 1978 to 1984, he was employed as a consultant by an important tour operator, and travelled all over Italy giving help and guidance to the chefs and cooks of the various holiday establishments.

In 1984, lured by the call of the sea, he joined Princess Cruises as sous

Alfredo Marzi

Silvestro Pernice

Pietro Roffo

Mario Rotti

Francesco Scarpati

Elio Vitiello

chef and was soon named master chef.

Chef Cereda makes his home in Armeno. He is married to Daniela Tonati, and they have a son, Francesco.

GIAMPAOLO MARCHI

Giampaolo Marchi, chef de cuisine, was born in 1940 in the city of Ameglia, La Spezia. He now lives in Lerici.

Chef Marchi attended the professional hotel school in La Spezia, where he finished his studies at the age of 16. He then started working on cargo ships as a galley boy in the kitchens. At the age of 19, Chef Marchi began working at the Grand Hotel of Courmayeur as sous chef. One year later, he re-embarked on cargo ships as a cook and worked in the provision department for four years.

In 1976 he received his certification as the director of the kitchen, and in 1982 he was fully promoted to executive chef with Princess Cruises.

ALFREDO MARZI

Alfredo Marzi is the youngest of six sons in a family of illustrious chefs with high standards. By the time he was 12, he was so impressed by his brothers' tales of life in the big hotels that he, too, decided on a chef's career.

Chef Marzi began his training in 1961 and joined Princess Cruises in 1977. He served five years on the Royal Princess and five years on the Island Princess before heading up the Sky Princess galley, where he is now executive chef.

Chef Marzi's achievements were recognized recently at the biennial competition, Decibels d'Auguste Escoffier, in Paris, where he won the culinary world's equivalent of an Oscar.

SILVESTRO PERNICE

Silvestro Pernice's birthplace was Torre Del Greco, Naples, where he resides today with his wife, Maria, and their two sons.

After graduating from junior high school, he began his professional training at the Hotel Dei Congressi.

He began his career as sous chef at the Plaza in Rome and later moved to the restaurant Pentolaccia in Sorrento.

He went to sea in 1960 and became executive chef of the Fair Princess in 1981.

PIETRO ROFFO

Pietro Roffo was born and raised in Lerici. He was educated at the Nautical Institute and at the hotel school in Lerici. When Chef Roffo is off duty, he lives in Lerici with his wife and daughter. He enjoys playing golf and reading poetry.

After extensive experience in hotels and on cruise ships, he came to Princess Cruises in 1974 at the age of 35, and rapidly rose from first cook to sous chef and then to his present position of chef.

— *(continued on next page)* —

139

140

MARIO ROTTI
Mario Rotti was born in Valduggia in 1942. He attended hotel school in Borgosesia, and his first position was as an assistant cook in the Hotel Tre Re in 1957. After serving as a cook in various hotels and Italian cruise ships, he came to the United States in 1970, where he was a chef in restaurants in Palm Beach, Florida and Westhampton, Long Island.

He is a member of La Chaine des Rotisseurs, the world's oldest culinary society, and the Italian Cook Association. Chef Rotti won first- and second-place prizes in the San Francisco Pier 39 "Olympic Crab Contest" in 1982 and 1983, respectively.

Chef Rotti joined Princess Cruises in 1973.

FRANCESCO SCARPATI
Genova was Francesco Scarpati's birthplace, and that is where he makes his home with his wife, Amalia, and two sons.

After finishing junior high school in 1950, Chef Scarpati's career began on a luxury cruise ship where he rose to assistant executive chef.

In 1974, he moved to the United States for two years, serving as executive chef in several well-known New York restaurants.

Following a stint as executive chef with other luxury cruise ships, he now brings the fruits of his long and varied experience to Princess Cruises as executive chef.

ELIO VITIELLO
Another award-winning Princess Cruises chef, Elio Vitiello is the proud winner of two gastronomic competitions in Turin: Atlantic Hotel, and Berretto D'Oro.

Since 1970 he has been chef de cuisine, starting with his first appointment, at sea with Società Italia. From 1980 to 1984 he was a teacher of the hotel trade. Then, in 1984, Vitiello joined Princess Cruises to serve as executive chef.

Chef Vitiello was born in Genova in 1933. He is married to Cabona Rosetta, and they have a daughter, Cinzia. When he is not travelling to far-off places on a Princess Cruises ship, he enjoys his hobby, ham radio operation.

RECIPE INDEX

143

ACKNOWLEDGMENTS AND CREDITS

144

Special thanks to the following Princess Cruises personnel whose assistance was immeasurable in the making of this book:

Aldo Marchi

Dr. G. Gallizio

Dennis LeVine

Omar Silingardi

Mary Ann Cavano

Susan Mulligan

Editorial:
  Marilyn Kostick
  Editor / Dorison House Publishers, *Boston, Massachusetts*
Art Direction, Book Design and Typography:
  Myra Lee Conway / Design, *Brockton, Massachusetts*
Photography:
  Corinne Colen Photography, *New York City, New York*
Assistant Photographers:
  Kari Anderson, *Clifton, New Jersey*
  Steve Adams, *New York City, New York*
Food Stylist:
  Rick Ellis, *New York City, New York*
Assistant Food Stylists:
  William Smith, *Brooklyn, New York*
  Cynthia W. Caldwell, *Northampton, Massachusetts*
Prop Stylist:
  Linda Cheverton-Wick, *New York City, New York*
Manuscript Consultants:
  Dorothy Crandall
  Beth Gibson
  Elizabeth Lowell
  Joanne Tribulauskas

Crystal stemware throughout this book by Baccarat, 625 Madison Avenue, New York City, New York.

Cover: China, Granite Verte, at Thaxton & Company, 780 Madison Avenue, New York City. Sterling silver flatware from Thaxton & Company.

Page 5: China by Gien, at Baccarat.

Page 25: Baccarat crystal bowls and underplates, at Baccarat.

Page 28: Plate by Gien, at Baccarat.

Page 71: Pompeii China, by Puiforcat, at Baccarat.

Page 79: China by Ceralene, at Baccarat.

Page 83: China by Ceralene, at Baccarat. Sterling silver, from Thaxton & Company.

Page 109: China by Gien, at Baccarat.

Page 118: China by Gien, at Baccarat.

Page 123: China by Puiforcat, at Baccarat.

Page 129: Plate by Ceralene, at Baccarat.